ROAD MAP FOR DEVELOPING AN ONLINE PLATFORM TO TRADE NONPERFORMING LOANS IN ASIA AND THE PACIFIC

OCTOBER 2022

ADB

ASIAN DEVELOPMENT BANK

© 2022 Asian Development Bank
6 ADB Avenue, Mandaluyong City, 1550 Metro Manila, Philippines
Tel +63 2 8632 4444; Fax +63 2 8636 2444
www.adb.org

Some rights reserved. Published in 2022.

ISBN 978-92-9269-789-1 (print); 978-92-9269-790-7 (electronic); 978-92-9269-791-4 (ebook)
Publication Stock No. TCS220434-2
DOI: http://dx.doi.org/10.22617/TCS220434-2

Notes:
1. In this publication, "$" refers to United States dollars, "CNY" to Chinese yuan, and "RM" to Malaysian ringgit.
2. ADB recognizes "China" as the People's Republic of China, "Korea" as the Republic of Korea, and "Vietnam" as Viet Nam.

Cover design by Francis Manio.

Printed on recycled paper

Contents

Tables, Figures, and Boxes   v

Foreword   vi

Acknowledgments   vii

Abbreviations   viii

Executive Summary   ix

I.   Overview of Nonperforming Loan Markets in Asia   **1**
    A.   Introduction   1
    B.   Report Structure   1
    C.   Asia in Overview   2

II.   Methodological Approach   **17**
    A.   Potential Benefits of Online Nonperforming Loan Platforms   18
    B.   Nonperforming Loan Transaction Lifecycle   19
    C.   Prerequisites for a Functioning Secondary Market for Nonperforming Loans   24

III.   Criteria for Assessment of Identified Economies' Capacity for Nonperforming Loan Trading   **27**

IV.   Feasibility for Nonperforming Loan Trading   **32**
    A.   Existing and Possible Legal Requisites and Conditions for Nonperforming Loan Trading   32
    B.   Overview of Current Policies and Mechanisms on Sale of Nonperforming Loans   34
        to Foreign Investors and Cross-Border Trading
    C.   Nonperforming Loan Recognition and Valuation Standards   35
    D.   Servicing Infrastructure   35
    E.   Legal Framework for Nonperforming Loans Securitization   37
    F.   Legal Foundation of Asset Management Companies to Realize Profits   37
        from Intermediating Nonperforming Loans Sales to Foreign Investors
    G.   Relationship and Dynamics between Platform Founders or Operators   38
        and Platform Participants

V.   Practical Considerations in Developing a Nonperforming Loan Platform   **39**
    A.   Functionality and Ancillary Services   39
    B.   Geographic Reach   40
    C.   Asset Perimeter   40

D.   Data Consistency (Templates)   41
E.   Data Quality—Financial Data   43
F.   Availability of Nonfinancial Data for Due Diligence   44
G.   Ownership   44
H.   Governance   46
I.   Incentives for Using an Online Platform and Other Considerations   46
J.   Road Map for the Development of Nonperforming Loan Markets   47
       in the Region and an Online Nonperforming Loan Trading Platform

Appendix: List of Partners in the Conduct of Interviews and Survey   **49**

References   **50**

Tables, Figures, and Boxes

Tables

1	Gross Domestic Product Growth Rate, Selected Economies	3
2	Asian Banking Sector Nonperforming Loans, 2011–2021	4
3	Summary of Nonperforming Loan Classification Methodologies Adopted in Studied Countries	6
4	World Bank—Insolvency Regime Effectiveness	9
5	Summary of Nonperforming Loan Secondary Market for Studied Countries in Asia	11
6	Asset Classes Traded on Online Platforms in Asia	16
7	Nonperforming Loan Transaction Lifecycle—Seller's Perspective Illustrative	21
8	Typical Data Tape Fields	22
9	Illustrative Scoring Basis	29
10	Illustrative Rankings of Readiness for an Online Nonperforming Loan Transaction Platform	30
11	Country Summary for Existing and Possible Legal Requisites and Conditions for Nonperforming Loan Trading	33
12	Nonperforming Loan Market Activity	34
13	Considerations by Asset Type	40
14	Alternative Ownership Models—Pros and Cons	45
15	Key Principles for the Development of Nonperforming Loan Markets and an Online Trading Platform	48

Figures

1	Nonperforming Loan Levels by Country	8
2	Nonperforming Loan Platforms—Functionalities, Full-Service Offering	14
3	Typical Online Trading Platform Process	15
4	Nonperforming Loan Transaction Volumes, Europe, and the People's Republic of China, 2018–2020 Comparison	19
5	Illustrative Nonperforming Loan Transaction—Simplified Process	20
6	Typical Nonperforming Loan Documentation Requirements for Investor Due Diligence	23
7	Typical Process for Document Extraction	23
8	Features of Underdeveloped Secondary Markets	24
9	Bid-Ask Spreads in Asia—Difference between Net Book Value and Estimated Bid Price	27

Boxes

1	Case Study—People's Republic of China	13
2	European Banking Authority Data Templates	42

Foreword

The aftermath of the coronavirus disease (COVID-19) pandemic, the Russian Invasion of Ukraine, and global monetary tightening are raising uncertainties about global and regional financial conditions. Higher debt levels in many countries and deteriorating credit quality have aggravated the situation, putting the region's financial systems at risk. Against this backdrop, a sharp increase in nonperforming loans (NPLs) could destabilize the region's banking and financial systems and compromise a post-pandemic and sustained economic recovery. By end-2021, NPLs held by banks in the region were already considerably higher than pre-COVID-19 levels, and these could worsen as troubles persist and as many central banks hike interest rates to tame inflation.

A developed market for NPL trading can effectively help reduce NPLs in banking systems by mobilizing private capital to relieve distressed bank assets. Indeed, development and deepening of NPL markets was already on the policy agenda before COVID-19. The current economic and financial challenges only underscore the relevance of this strategy to facilitate swift resolution of banks' NPLs.

A silver lining of the pandemic has been the accelerated adoption of digital solutions across economies. In fact, digital technology has transformed financial systems worldwide, producing noticeably greater efficiency and transparency by promoting information flows, reducing operational and transactional costs, and improving financial inclusion. As such, an online NPL trading platform could help further develop NPL markets in the region by bringing together buyers, sellers, and service providers in a digital marketplace. It could streamline the overall transaction process and address some of the supply-side, demand-side, and structural impediments weighing on the smooth functioning of NPL markets.

To this end, this report examines the feasibility of establishing an online NPL transaction platform in Asia and the Pacific as an additional tool for resolving NPLs. It (i) examines the state and level of development of Asia's NPL markets; (ii) discusses benefits, functions, and practical considerations of an electronic NPL trading platform; (iii) assesses countries' readiness for an electronic platform; and (iv) proposes a road map for the development of NPL markets in the region and of an online NPL trading platform.

I hope this report can serve as a useful reference for the development of the region's NPL markets. I am also confident that the road map can help guide policy actions that will advance regional NPL markets and hence strengthen financial stability.

Albert Francis Park
Chief Economist and Director General
Economic Research and Regional Cooperation Department
Asian Development Bank

Acknowledgments

This report was prepared by the Regional Cooperation and Integration Division of the Economic Research and Regional Cooperation Department of the Asian Development Bank (ADB). The report development was supported by knowledge and support technical assistance (TA) 9210: Enhancing Research Alliance and South–South Development Policy Cooperation Between Asia and the Pacific and Latin America, financed by ADB's technical assistance special fund; while the report production was supported by TA 9497: Strengthening Asia's Financial Safety Nets and Resolution Mechanisms, financed by ADB's technical assistance special fund, the People's Republic of China Poverty Reduction and Regional Cooperation Fund, and the Republic of Korea e-Asia and Knowledge Partnership Fund.

Under the overall direction and guidance of Regional Cooperation and Integration Division Director Cyn-Young Park, the preparation of the report was led by Peter Rosenkranz and Paulo Rodelio Halili. Main authors of the report are Richard Bevan and Peter Rosenkranz. Background research and analysis have been prepared by Altynai Kelgenbaeva, Vikki Lin, and Lily Hao.

The report greatly benefited from comments and suggestions received from Sun Joon Choe, Alok Gahrotra, Giacomo Giannetto, Manohari Gunawardhena, Aziz Haydarov, Junkyu Lee, Reiner Martin, and Stephen Schuster.

The report team greatly acknowledges the support by the following partners for helpful insights during report preparation stemming from interviews and surveys: China Great Wall Asset Management Company; Debt and Asset Trading Corporation; European Banking Authority; First Financial Network, Inc.; Fund for Problem Loans; International Finance Corporation; Korean Asset Management Company; Sukhumvit Asset Management; Viet Nam Asset Management Company; and Zheshang Asset Management Company.

The report team is also grateful for the helpful feedback provided by participants of the following events: the Regional Cooperation and Integration Policy Open Dialogue: Strengthening Asia's NPL Markets Through Transaction Platforms held on 7 April 2021, and the 7th International Public Asset Management Companies Forum Training Seminar on Seeking New Mechanism Addressing an Upsurge of Nonperforming Loans in Post-COVID-19 Era conducted on 20–23 June 2022.

Eric Van Zant edited the manuscript, Francis Manio created the cover design, and Alfredo de Jesus implemented the typesetting and layout. Joy Quitazol-Gonzalez proofread the report, while Marjorie Celis handled the page proof checking, with assistance from Carol Ongchangco. The Printing Services Unit of ADB's Corporate Services Department and the Publishing Team of the Department of Communications supported printing and publishing.

Abbreviations

ADB	Asian Development Bank
AMC	asset management company
COVID-19	coronavirus disease
EBA	European Banking Authority
NPL	nonperforming loan
PRC	People's Republic of China
SMEs	small and medium-sized enterprises
US	United States

Executive Summary

Overview of the Nonperforming Loan Market in Asia and the Pacific

The coronavirus disease (COVID-19) pandemic has hit businesses and economies around the world, albeit in varying degrees. In Asia and the Pacific, this has added to strains on bank asset quality, raising the risk of higher nonperforming loans (NPLs) and adverse macrofinancial consequences. As at the end of 2021, NPLs held by banking institutions across the region increased to over $805 billion, from $703 billion in 2019 ($772 billion in 2020),[1] as the pandemic and measures designed to control it disrupted national economies. Indeed, this may even considerably underestimate the level, in that the deterioration in loan asset quality might have been obscured by government-led policy responses such as debt moratoria and regulatory forbearance. The full extent of increased NPLs may not be known for some time and forecasts may get adjusted; in October 2020, Moody's,[2] the credit rating agency, forecast NPLs to double on average across 14 key Asia and the Pacific economies by 2022, as COVID-19 relief measures are unwound.

A deterioration in credit quality is recognized as a significant risk for many markets in the region and indeed more broadly. High NPL ratios increase banks' capital requirements and funding costs and act as a brake on further lending into the real economy, tying up other scarce resources, including human capital, which could yet disrupt the post-pandemic economic recovery.

Benefits of Well-Functioning Nonperforming Loan Markets

Well-developed markets for NPLs have multiple benefits for central banks and regulators charged with managing financial stability. They are also good for banks facing high stocks of NPLs wanting to engage in NPL portfolio sales strategies (direct sales or securitizations) to clean up their balance sheets and generate external capital, including from foreign investors, which makes them more resilient and better able to absorb losses. As such, they also act as a powerful tool in managing broader macrofinancial risks and driving economic recovery.

Against the backdrop that, in several Asian countries, public asset management companies are significant buyers of NPLs from banks, further developing NPL secondary markets in the region, while amply protecting borrowers

---

[1]   Data are from the International Monetary Fund, central banks, and prudential authorities. The figure only includes economies with the latest gross NPL stock of over $500 million. For 2021, we use the third quarter (Q3) and/or Q4 levels applied for all countries—except Japan, where we use Q1; and Viet Nam, Sri Lanka, and Kazakhstan, where we use Q2.

[2]   Moody's Investors Service. 2020. Moody's - Risks Rise Substantially for APAC Banks, But Credit Profiles Remain Broadly Intact. Research Announcement. 6 October.

from oppressive collection practices,[3] would substantially support collective efforts to tackle the potential rise in impaired loans ahead. This might also provide benefits beyond NPLs, including sales of noncore assets.

When combined with a well-developed independent loan servicing industry, it could also ameliorate the potential moral hazard issue as risk exposures are transferred and managed by third-party specialists instead of the originating banks.

Assessment of Nonperforming Loan Market Development and Readiness for an Online Nonperforming Loan Platform

Despite notable exceptions in recent years, NPL markets remain largely underdeveloped in Asia. Liquidity and depth remain modest and bid-ask spreads rather high. In addition, regulatory impediments hamper NPL trading.

Many economies in the region, particularly the People's Republic of China (PRC), Thailand, the Republic of Korea, Indonesia, and Kazakhstan, may benefit greatly from the development of an online NPL trading platform as an additional tool for NPL resolution.[4] But countries' readiness varies substantially, with the PRC, Thailand, and the Republic of Korea more advanced than others in terms of NPL trading ecosystems (e.g., supportive legal system, loan servicing capacity, among other factors). Additionally, the Kazakhstan and Viet Nam governments intend to investigate the steps necessary to develop NPL markets, including cross-border trading and the development of an online NPL trading platform.

Potential Benefits of Online Nonperforming Loan Platforms

Against this background, online auction platforms are generally considered to have significant potential to broaden the channels for NPL disposal and break down geographical boundaries.[5]

Transaction platforms may facilitate and maintain active, liquid, and efficient secondary markets for NPLs, in the same way as digital retail platforms have for consumer goods. In the COVID-19 context, as an online marketplace with all necessary documentation digitized, these would be able to function better, notwithstanding external conditions.

---

[3] That is, collection practices, which may include threatening or intimidating behavior.
[4] Malaysia was also studied; NPL stocks in that country are relatively low, and compared to other countries, may be less interesting to foreign investors.
[5] For example, see: European Commission. 2018. Communication from the Commission to the European Parliament, the Council and the European Central Bank: First Progress Report on the Reduction of Non-Performing Loans in Europe. *Commission Staff Working Document*. No. 33. Brussels.

Functionalities of Online Nonperforming Loan Platforms

A full range of functionalities could maximize the benefits of an online NPL transaction platform, by matching buyers and sellers to data warehousing and analytics, through online bidding, and from ancillary services. When developing a platform, it may not be necessary to introduce these all at once. Rather, platforms could be built on a modular basis—starting with transaction facilitation, data review, and validation—perhaps an essential requirement to build trust in the platform and adding extra modalities over time. This is likely to be a quicker process than developing a full service offering and allowing earlier recognition of the potential benefits.

The matrix below sets out typical functionalities of NPL online platforms, which could be the template for the development of a platform in Asia.

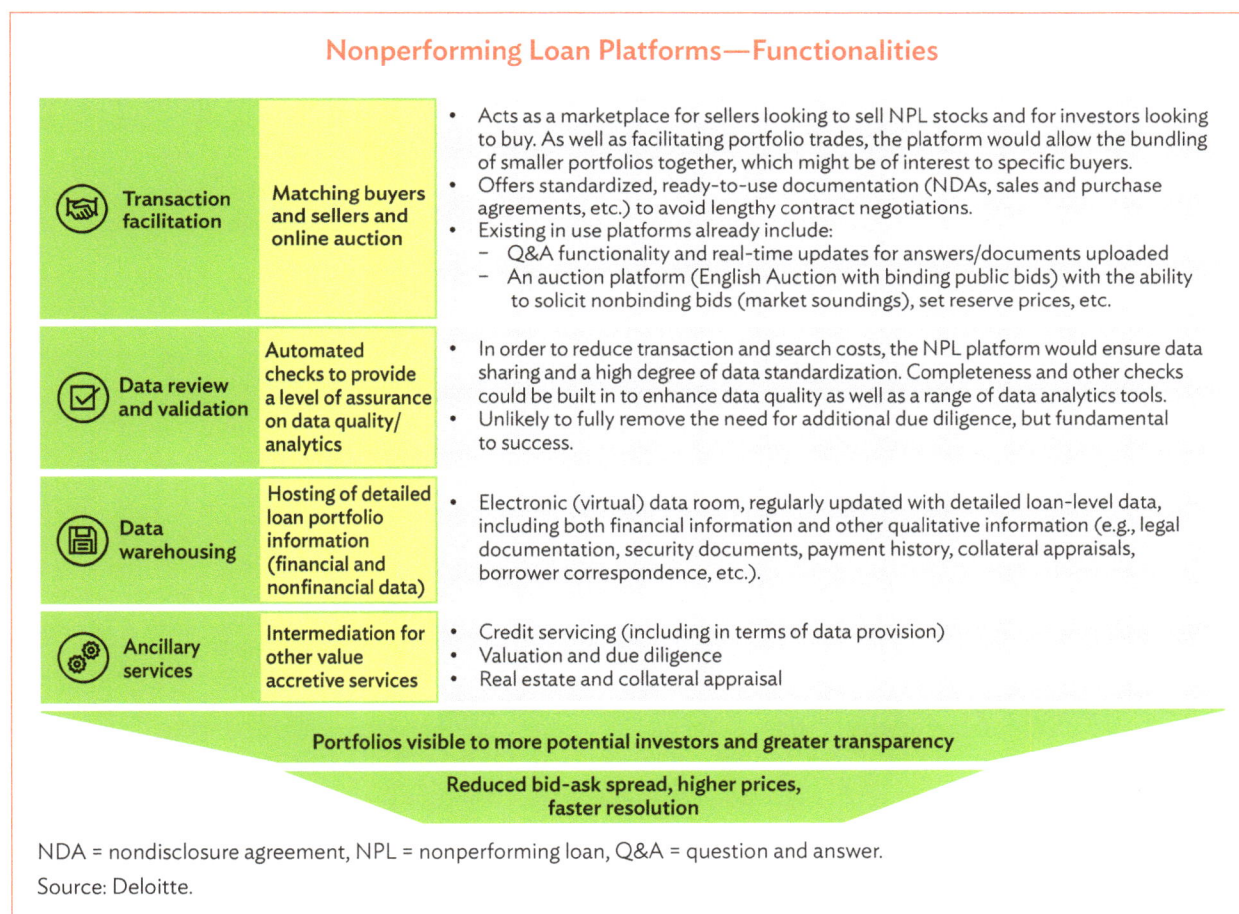

Nonperforming Loan Platforms—Functionalities

Transaction facilitation	**Matching buyers and sellers and online auction**	• Acts as a marketplace for sellers looking to sell NPL stocks and for investors looking to buy. As well as facilitating portfolio trades, the platform would allow the bundling of smaller portfolios together, which might be of interest to specific buyers.
		• Offers standardized, ready-to-use documentation (NDAs, sales and purchase agreements, etc.) to avoid lengthy contract negotiations.
		• Existing in use platforms already include:
		  – Q&A functionality and real-time updates for answers/documents uploaded
		  – An auction platform (English Auction with binding public bids) with the ability to solicit nonbinding bids (market soundings), set reserve prices, etc.

Data review and validation	**Automated checks to provide a level of assurance on data quality/ analytics**	• In order to reduce transaction and search costs, the NPL platform would ensure data sharing and a high degree of data standardization. Completeness and other checks could be built in to enhance data quality as well as a range of data analytics tools. • Unlikely to fully remove the need for additional due diligence, but fundamental to success.
Data warehousing	**Hosting of detailed loan portfolio information (financial and nonfinancial data)**	• Electronic (virtual) data room, regularly updated with detailed loan-level data, including both financial information and other qualitative information (e.g., legal documentation, security documents, payment history, collateral appraisals, borrower correspondence, etc.).
Ancillary services	**Intermediation for other value accretive services**	• Credit servicing (including in terms of data provision) • Valuation and due diligence • Real estate and collateral appraisal

Portfolios visible to more potential investors and greater transparency

Reduced bid-ask spread, higher prices, faster resolution

NDA = nondisclosure agreement, NPL = nonperforming loan, Q&A = question and answer.
Source: Deloitte.

For holders of NPLs and prospective purchasers, transaction platforms would help reduce the degree of dysfunction in markets for NPLs, helping address information asymmetries, increase creditor coordination, and broaden the investor base. This would lead to more developed and liquid NPL markets, with better pricing mechanisms.

Practical Considerations

Geographic reach

The potential benefits of transaction platforms, in keeping transaction costs low and broadening market reach, might be best achieved by maximizing the number of users and driving economies of scale. This implies that, for some smaller markets at least, a platform capable of dealing with transactions on a regional basis should be the overall objective. In this way, sellers of NPLs in smaller markets, which otherwise might not attract significant investor interest, could potentially bundle their NPLs with other loans (e.g., by sector) to create larger, more saleable portfolios.

That said, NPL markets in different jurisdictions are not all at the same stages of development, with some countries potentially requiring significant legal reforms, including to collateral enforcement and asset ownership to attract investors and create a functioning market. As such, development of a regional platform may best be attempted in stages, focusing first on those countries ready for it (e.g., the PRC, the Republic of Korea, Thailand, etc.) with other countries joining later, when ready. In the meantime, this should not prevent individual countries from developing domestic platforms.

Moreover, there is no apparent overriding reason that only one platform should be developed to transact NPL disposals. Subject to issues around achieving critical mass and a sufficient number of users, an alternative option could be the development of a regional network of platforms, sharing common standards on best practice operation and information disclosure and cooperating with each other to maximize reach and number of transactions.

Asset perimeter

For similar reasons, it seems appropriate to aim for as broad a scope of assets traded on the platform as possible. Indeed, there is no reason noncore assets generally (i.e., not just NPLs), including performing portfolios, could not be offered on the platform. In fact, many portfolio sales are a mix of performing and nonperforming or reperforming loans.

Data consistency (templates)

A key objective of the platform is to reduce information asymmetries and lower transaction costs, thereby mitigating potential barriers to entry and opening up the NPL market in the region to a broader investor base, including smaller investors who might otherwise find themselves priced out by high due diligence costs.

Standardized data templates, prepared by the seller and drawn from underlying bank systems and data types, can help with this. This can enhance granularity, quality, and comparability of NPL data and increase transparency. Cost savings can be achieved through a more efficient and smoother due diligence process. Buyers get the information they need and sellers know, up front, what information is expected and can, therefore, incorporate it into their loan systems architecture.

At the same time, standardized templates create a level playing field between different platform operators, fostering fairer competition, and setting a minimum standard for information provision.

The European Banking Authority's revised NPL template proposals (currently under discussion) provide a potential starting point (EBA 2021). These recognize that information requirements may differ by jurisdiction (given different regulation); hence, some tailoring to different markets may be needed.

As suggested in the consultation paper, the templates could include certain minimum levels of information (i.e., required for all loans), with additional fields required for completion if certain size criteria are triggered (e.g., for larger loans above an agreed threshold). Country-specific requirements could be dealt with in the same way.

Should the template be voluntary or mandatory? Requiring market participants to use a standard information template would foster harmonization and generate process efficiencies, reducing overall transaction costs.

As noted, in addition to providing a level of "generic" information common to all portfolios (distinguished by asset class), additional country-specific fields may be required to cater for local legal requirements. The templates would not necessarily be tied to regulatory reporting. When designing the templates, there would be benefits in working alongside regulators to reduce the new information required and, thereby, minimize cost implications to banks needing to complete the template.

As such, it is important that requirements are kept proportionate to what is actually required for pricing and due diligence (as opposed to what is "nice to have") and to what banks can actually produce.

Given the early stage of development of NPL markets in certain Asian countries, harmonizing data requirements through a standardized NPL template may be easier to achieve than in other, more mature markets, with a number of platforms already in operation, where there may be a natural reluctance to having to remodel existing practices.

Should templates be used for new NPLs only or also for existing stocks? The templates would form the basis for information stored on the transaction platform and their use would be a requirement for use of the platform.

Templates could also form the basis for a centralized NPL (post trade) data depository for analyzing and monitoring overall NPL lifecycle evolution, which could be useful in developing NPL markets more generally (i.e., understanding trends and strategies better). This is currently being considered by the European Commission (EC 2020). This would also provide central banks, supervisors, and other policy makers beneficial data for financial stability analysis.

Using templates more broadly may also provide macrofinancial benefits (i.e., regardless whether NPLs are to be sold on the platform); given the cost of preparation on banks and financial institutions, this would be a secondary objective and would require separate cost-benefit evaluation.

Who should take the lead in developing the templates and harmonizing data requirements? Asia does not have the same framework of supranational organizations as other regions. However, coordinating design standards across jurisdictions is a central task that is perhaps best done either by an international development organization or a multinational industry body, requiring the sponsorship of regional governments, regulators, and central banks, all of which will have a fundamental role to play.

Data quality—financial data

Information loaded onto the platform needs to be of good quality to build trust in the platform and to keep due diligence costs low. Prior to uploading on the platform, NPL data should be subject to a minimum level of data verification and validation to ensure accuracy and fitness for purpose.

Availability of nonfinancial data for due diligence

Investors rely on financial and nonfinancial data for due diligence. For nonfinancial data, in many cases, documents may have to be manually extracted, cleansed, and catalogued, making for a potentially very labor-intensive process, particularly for large loan portfolios with a significant number of underlying borrowers. Thereafter, for a fully online NPL platform, this would need to be digitized and uploaded. Alternatively, the platform could operate to include just the basic financial data, as required for initial due diligence and buyer evaluation, with more detailed financial and nonfinancial data made available by the seller as required.

Ownership

Several alternatives exist, dependent on whether the platform is set up as a single regional platform or by individual nations on a domestic basis only.

On balance, given their ability to drive efficiencies and best practices, platforms owned by the private sector may represent an optimum model. But governments have an important role to play, individually and jointly, particularly in the early stages of development in implementing necessary legal reforms and providing incentives to buyers and sellers. This is further explained in Chapter V, section G (pp. 44–45).

Creating a market for cross-border transactions will require collaboration and the agreement of minimum common standards. International development organizations could play an important role in this, as standard setters. Compliance with such standards would earn the platform a "seal of approval," which could be beneficial in building user confidence. Alternatively, an industry-wide independent standard setter for the region could be established. A number of industry bodies already exist in the region and the extension of their remit could be considered as an option.

Governance

Platforms would need to comply with all appropriate national laws and regulations of the countries in which they operate.

Consistent with transaction platforms already in use, an online NPL platform would not provide settlement services or be part of the legal contracting process, all of which would take place off-platform, on a bilateral basis between the parties.[6] Nor would the platform ever "own" the assets.

As such, platforms would not represent financial market infrastructure and would not typically be regulated. Nevertheless, dependent on the services offered, accredited platforms would be subject to the governance requirements and standards set by the body granting the "seal of approval." Further consideration of regulatory requirements would likely be needed for the design and planning of online platforms.

---

[6]   A network of platforms working under common standards could drive the same benefits.

Incentives for using an online transaction platform and other considerations

Aside from general incentives for banks to deleverage, including in terms of reduced capital requirements and improved liquidity, online NPL transaction platforms offer potentially significant process benefits to users including:

- wider and deeper channels to market and better matching between buyers and sellers;
- faster execution (anecdotally, existing platform operators talk about between 55% and 90% reduction in times compared to offline processes);
- lower transaction costs; and
- better pricing compared to offline disposals.

For asset management companies, these factors would be of considerable benefit in addressing potential liquidity issues, which (as commented on by participants in this study) represent a limiting factor in pursuing their financial stability mandate.

Additionally, and reflecting overall financial stability benefits in terms of better information for policymaking, it may be appropriate to consider fiscal incentives for the use of NPL data templates as part of the development of an online platform.

Fees

Fee structures should be transparent and set at levels affordable to users, regardless of size, so as not to act as a disincentive to smaller buyers or sellers. Ultimately, rates need to be commercially viable to the operators, and low fee levels are only possible with a critical mass of users. Initially, during the ramp-up phase, some level of subsidy, public support, or investment may be necessary.

Road Map For Developing an Online Platform to Trade Nonperforming Loans in the Region

Development of an online platform to transact NPLs in the region, including on a cross border basis, is a significant undertaking. Moreover, not all countries in the region are at the same state of development in terms of market maturity and infrastructure, with a number requiring potentially significant legal and other reforms, which could take several years to achieve. It may not be necessary or even desirable to wait for all countries in the region to reach the required same level of market development before undertaking further work. Rather, countries meeting the required criteria could initiate the development programme first, with others joining later when conditions are met.

Considering what form the platform takes, a network of platforms could be an alternative to a single regional platform, sharing common standards in best practice operation and information disclosure, and cooperating with each other to maximize reach and the overall market penetration.

The following guiding principles and initial actions may help guide the development of an online trading platform for the region and the further development of the NPL market on both domestic and cross-border bases:

Key Guiding Principles for Development of an Online Nonperforming Loan Trading Platform

Proposed Guiding Principles
Consistent nonperforming loan (NPL) recognition standards and valuation methodologies—a precondition for trading NPLs on the platform (and general market development) would be the adoption of agreed international standards for NPL recognition and valuation methodologies. While many countries have adopted the International Financial Reporting Standards, not all have. Given their broader financial stability to remit and significant levels of alignment, central banks and regulators may be expected to play an important role in promoting this, as well as from a general sponsorship perspective.
Level playing field—NPL markets and platforms should be regulated on a nondiscriminatory basis, with the same standards and regulatory requirements applying to both foreign and domestic NPL investors. Currently, this is not always the case, which creates regulatory uncertainty and is a barrier to investment.
A level of minimum standards should be developed both in NPL markets generally and online NPL platforms. This could be in the form of best practice guidelines and data quality, which would foster confidence and encourage broader market participation.
Balanced protection for consumers—considering loan servicing and debt collection, regulators need to balance appropriate and sustainable collection practices, which protect consumers and borrowers, and industry standards that do not restrict lenders' ability to efficiently work out NPLs.

Source: Authors' compilation.

As a near-term next step, broader consultation would be beneficial. Notably, several international development organizations are also looking at this and additional insights may be helpful. The initiative should likewise be of considerable interest to central banks and regulators in the region charged with managing financial stability. Central banks and regulators will also have a key role to play in removing roadblocks both to the development of NPL markets and in NPL online platforms. Consultations could also include private sector platform operators (inside and outside Asia) so as to impart lessons from practical experience, as well as potential users of the platform (holders of NPL stocks and investors) and industry representatives.

Areas for further consideration and consultation might include:

- development of appropriate best practice guidance for NPL management and disposals (e.g., along the lines of the guidance that the European Commission has announced it is intending to develop, in conjunction with the European Banking Authority) (EC 2020);
- minimum standard setting; and
- harmonized data templates for NPL transactions.

I. Overview of Nonperforming Loan Markets in Asia

A. Introduction

The coronavirus disease (COVID-19) pandemic has hurt global and regional markets and operating conditions, but government support measures and liquidity have limited the degree of credit deterioration to date. However, credit quality could deteriorate when this temporary financial relief is lifted and regulatory forbearance phased out, highlighting the risks of rising nonperforming loans (NPLs). Previous crisis experiences have illustrated the negative macrofinancial effects NPLs can have on the real economy, underlining the importance of swift action to reduce high NPLs. A sharp increase in NPLs could destabilize regional financial systems and compromise the post-pandemic economic recovery.

Developing a marketplace for NPL trading can be an effective measure to relieve banks of their NPLs, and thus ensure their capacity for financial intermediation, which might otherwise be disrupted. While development and deepening of NPL markets were already on the policy agenda even prior to COVID-19, the pandemic underscores its relevance to facilitate the swift resolution of banks' NPLs. Against this backdrop, the Asian Development Bank (ADB) has launched a knowledge project to examine the feasibility of establishing an NPL transaction platform for the Asia and Pacific region as an additional tool for resolving NPLs.

B. Report Structure

Chapter I sets out the background to the study and provides a regional NPL overview, including

- An analysis of NPL levels and market trends in the region against the backdrop of COVID-19, including potential future trends;
- An overview of existing online NPL or public asset disposal systems being used by governments and/or public agencies in the region;
- A breakdown of outstanding NPLs, valuation methodologies, resolution practices, and typical court auction procedures by country assessed; and
- An overview of the role of asset management companies (AMCs) in resolving NPLs in the region.

Chapter II starts with methodological approach and comments on the potential benefits of online NPL platforms to further develop secondary markets in the region. It reviews the NPL transaction lifecycle and looks at how these can be adapted to online trading and the prerequisites for a functioning NPL market, featuring narrowed bid-ask spreads, a broad pool of investors, and capacity for cross-border trades.

Chapter III looks at relevant assessment criteria for determining countries' states of readiness, and Chapter IV considers selected markets' capacities and feasibility to engage in domestic NPL trading and possibly in cross-border transactions of distressed debts. This includes

- An overview of current policies and mechanisms on repatriation, incentivizing foreign investors, and restrictions, if any, on selling NPLs to foreign investors;
- An assessment of both existing and possible legal requisites and conditions for (online) NPL trading;
- An overview of the relative development of loan servicing infrastructure in selected countries as an important prerequisite for an efficient functioning secondary market;
- The legal foundation of AMCs to realize profits from intermediating NPL sales to foreign investors;
- The possibility of foreign investor participation by appointing an agency or establishing a special purpose vehicle;
- The ownership transfer of NPLs between creditors in selected countries;
- The legal framework for NPL securitization, if any, in selected countries; and
- The nature of the dynamics between platform founders/operators and platform participants.

Chapter V then considers the overall feasibility and key challenges in developing an NPL platform per market. This includes the following:

- Examples of existing platforms in use including discussion on asset focus; and
- Practical issues to be considered in developing online platforms:
  - data consistency and quality, including the features and benefits from standardized data templates (e.g., the European Banking Authority [EBA] NPL template);
  - data privacy, including for cross-border transactions and where data should be hosted;
  - governance;
  - ownership; and
  - any restriction on public AMCs' involvement in such an online NPL trading platform (as limited by mandates, business scope, regulatory requirements, among other areas).

Chapter V also includes a proposed "road map" of next steps for development of an online NPL platform in the region.

C.   Asia in Overview

The COVID-19 pandemic has been a health crisis and an unprecedented economic challenge. Although banks entered the crisis in a stronger position than during the 2008 global financial crisis, the magnitude of the worldwide COVID-19 lockdowns has had far-reaching impact on businesses and economies.

According to ADB's Asian Development Outlook, economic growth contracted across developing Asia in 2020, except in the People's Republic of China (PRC); Taipei,China; and Viet Nam (Table 1). Gross domestic product grew 2.2% in the PRC; 3.4% in Taipei,China; and 2.9% in Viet Nam. Economic growth generally rebounded in 2021, except for Viet Nam, which recorded a slight growth slowdown compared with 2022.

Developing Asia's economy rebounded by 6.9% in 2021, but the recovery is still largely incomplete in most of the region. Vaccination efforts have contributed to the turnaround, although emergence of new variants remains a potential cause for concern. The latest ADB forecasts (as of April 2022) suggest that growth in 2022 could be in the region of 5.2% (0.1 percentage points down on previous forecasts) and 5.3% in 2023, with significant regional and geographical differences in the pace of growth anticipated.

Table 1: Gross Domestic Product Growth Rate, Selected Economies
(% per year)

Economy	ADO Apr-22				Difference from ADO Sep-21	
	2020	2021	2022F	2023F	2021F	2022F
Central Asia	**-2.0**	**5.6**	**3.6**	**4.0**	**1.5**	**-0.6**
Kazakhstan	-2.5	4.0	3.7	3.9	0.6	0.0
East Asia	**1.8**	**7.6**	**4.7**	**4.5**	**0.0**	**-0.4**
Hong Kong, China	-6.5	6.4	2.0	3.7	0.2	-1.4
PRC	2.2	8.1	5.0	4.8	0.0	-0.5
Republic of Korea	-0.9	4.0	3.0	2.6	0.0	-0.1
Taipei,China	3.4	6.4	3.8	3.0	0.2	0.8
South Asia	**-5.2**	**8.3**	**7.0**	**7.4**	**-0.5**	**0.0**
India	-6.6	8.9	7.5	8.0	-1.1	0.0
Southeast Asia	**-3.2**	**2.9**	**4.9**	**5.2**	**-0.2**	**-0.1**
Indonesia	-2.1	3.7	5.0	5.2	0.2	0.2
Malaysia	-5.6	3.1	6.0	5.4	-1.6	-0.1
Philippines	-9.6	5.6	6.0	6.3	1.1	0.5
Singapore	-4.1	7.6	4.3	3.2	1.1	0.2
Thailand	-6.2	1.6	3.0	4.5	0.8	-0.9
Viet Nam	2.9	2.6	2.0	6.5	-1.2	-4.5
Pacific	**-6.0**	**-0.6**	**3.9**	**5.4**	**0.0**	**-0.9**
Developing Asia	**-0.8**	**6.9**	**5.2**	**5.3**	**-0.2**	**-0.1**

ADO = Asian Development Outlook, F = forecast, PRC = People's Republic of China.

Notes: Developing Asia refers to the 46 members of the Asian Development Bank (ADB) listed below by geographic group:

1. Central Asia comprises Armenia, Azerbaijan, Georgia, Kazakhstan, the Kyrgyz Republic, Tajikistan, Turkmenistan, and Uzbekistan.
2. East Asia comprises Hong Kong, China; Mongolia; the PRC; the Republic of Korea; and Taipei,China.
3. A fluid situation permits no estimates or forecasts for Afghanistan in 2021-2023.
4. South Asia comprises Afghanistan, Bangladesh, Bhutan, India, Maldives, Nepal, Pakistan, and Sri Lanka.
5. Southeast Asia comprises Brunei Darussalam, Cambodia, Indonesia, the Lao People's Democratic Republic, Malaysia, Myanmar, the Philippines, Singapore, Thailand, Timor-Leste, and Viet Nam.
6. The Pacific comprises the Cook Islands, the Federated States of Micronesia, Fiji, Kiribati, the Marshall Islands, Nauru, Niue, Palau, Papua New Guinea, Samoa, Solomon Islands, Tonga, Tuvalu, and Vanuatu.
7. ADB placed on hold its assistance in Afghanistan, effective 15 August 2021 (ADB. 2021. ADB Statement on Afghanistan. News release. 10 November).

Sources: ADB. 2021a. *Asian Development Outlook 2021 Update: Transforming Agriculture in Asia*. Manila; and ADB. 2022. *Asian Development Outlook 2022: Mobilizing Taxes for Development*. Manila.

Nonperforming Loan Levels

Following the global financial crisis, and with a handful of exceptions (Table 2), NPL ratios have been declining or remained broadly flat, as economies recovered since governments, regulators, and central banks implemented measures to increase bank resilience. Reflecting the regulatory frameworks that banks operate under, high NPL ratios increase their capital requirements and can limit lending into the real economy and tie up other scarce resources, including human capital at the same time.

Considering economies in the region by asset group, countries with higher average income levels tend to have better asset quality. High-income nations have generally maintained their NPL ratios below 2%, even during 2020 when the pandemic struck—except for Singapore where levels increased to 2.6% in 2020 from 2.0% in 2019 (Table 2), before moving back in 2021 to 2.3%. However, certain countries in the lower-middle income groups have seen high-single to double-digit ratios in recent years. Despite the pandemic, NPL ratios did not considerably pick up in 2021 (continuing to decline in some instances). One of the factors contributing to that trend might be regulatory forbearance measures in several countries, which resulted in limited recognition of new NPLs. Phasing out of these temporary measures in 2022 and beyond will likely result in increased NPLs.

Table 2: Asian Banking Sector Nonperforming Loans, 2011–2021

Movement of banking sector NPLs in Asia over the past decade (as % of gross loan)		Latest NPLs ($bn)	% subtotal	% total	2011	2012	2013	2014	2015	2016	2017	2018	2019	2020	2021
Asia	Income Group	805.1													
East Asia		573.1	100.0	71.2											
People's Republic of China	Upper Middle	447.9	78.2	55.6	1.0	1.0	1.0	1.2	1.7	1.7	1.7	1.8	1.9	1.8	1.7
Japan	High Income	114.6	20.0	14.2	2.9	3.0	2.9	2.5	2.1	1.9	1.7	1.5	1.4	1.4	1.5
Republic of Korea	High Income	9.8	1.7	1.2	1.4	1.3	1.8	1.6	1.8	1.4	1.2	1.0	0.8	0.6	0.5
Mongolia	Lower Middle	0.7	0.1	0.1	5.9	4.2	5.3	5.0	7.5	8.5	8.5	10.4	10.2	11.8	10.0
South Asia		124.5	100.0	15.5											
India	Lower Middle	109.6	88.1	13.6	2.7	3.4	4.0	4.3	5.9	9.2	10.0	9.5	9.2	7.7	6.9
Bangladesh	Lower Middle	11.8	9.5	1.5	6.1	10.0	8.9	9.7	8.3	9.2	9.3	10.3	9.3	7.7	8.2
Sri Lanka	Lower Middle	2.5	2.0	0.3	3.8	3.6	5.6	4.2	3.2	2.6	2.5	3.4	4.7	4.9	5.0
Nepal	Lower Middle	0.5	0.4	0.1	4.8	4.4	4.3	3.6	2.9	2.1	2.0	1.8	1.8	2.0	1.4
Southeast Asia		74.5	100.0	9.3											
Singapore	High Income	22.3	29.9	2.8	1.3	1.2	1.2	1.1	1.6	2.2	2.0	1.9	2.0	2.6	2.3
Thailand	Upper Middle	16.2	21.7	2.0	2.7	2.3	2.2	2.2	2.6	2.8	2.9	2.9	3.0	3.1	3.1
Indonesia	Upper Middle	12.7	17.0	1.6	2.1	1.8	1.7	2.1	2.4	2.9	2.6	2.3	2.4	2.8	3.0

continued on next page

Table 2 *continued*

		Latest NPLs ($bn)	% subtotal	% total	2011	2012	2013	2014	2015	2016	2017	2018	2019	2020	2021
Movement of banking sector NPLs in Asia over the past decade (as % of gross loan)															
Philippines	Lower Middle	9.5	12.8	1.2	N/A	N/A	2.8	2.3	2.1	1.9	1.7	1.8	2.0	3.6	4.4
Viet Nam	Lower Middle	6.3	8.4	0.8	3.1	4.1	3.6	3.3	2.6	2.5	2.0	1.9	1.6	2.1	1.7
Malaysia	Upper Middle	6.6	8.9	0.8	2.8	2.1	1.9%	1.7	1.6	1.6	1.6	1.5	1.5	1.6	1.5
Cambodia	Lower Middle	0.9	1.2	0.1	2.3	2.2	2.3	1.6	1.6	2.1	2.1	2.0	1.6	1.8	2.1
Pacific		23.9	100.0	3.0											
Australia	High Income	23.1	96.4	2.9	1.9	1.7	1.3	1.0%	0.9	0.9	0.8	0.8	0.9	1.1	1.0
New Zealand	High Income	0.9	3.6	0.1	N/A	N/A	N/A	N/A	N/A	N/A	N/A	0.5	0.6	0.6	0.3
Central and West Asia		9.0	100.0	1.1											
Pakistan	Lower Middle	5.1	56.9	0.6	16.2	14.5	13.0	12.3	11.4	10.1	8.4	8.0	8.6	9.2	8.3
Kazakhstan	Upper Middle	1.7	19.2	0.2	30.8	29.8	31.2	23.5	8.0	6.7	9.3	7.4	8.1	6.9	4.8
Uzbekistan	Lower Middle	1.7	18.8	0.2	0.7	3.1	2.8	2.1	1.5	0.7	1.2	1.3	1.5	2.1	5.7
Azerbaijan	Upper Middle	0.5	5.2	0.1	6.4	6.2	5.1	5.3	6.9	9.0	13.8	12.2	8.3	6.1	4.6

bn = billion, N/A = not applicable, NPL = nonperforming loan.

Notes: Original values are denominated in local currencies and converted to United States dollars ($), with exchange rates on relevant dates. The table only includes selected countries with the latest reported gross NPL stock of over $500 million as of 31 December 2021. Lower NPLs are shown in green and higher NPLs in dark brown on a graduated scale through the spectrum. Countries studied in blue text.

Sources: Statistics published by central banks; and International Monetary Fund. 2021. Financial Soundness Indicators. (accessed 28 March 2022).

Nonperforming Loan Classification

At the same time, caution should be taken with NPL figures as definitions are not yet fully aligned across Asia, with several key economies continuing to use incurred loss methodologies or simple time-based measures. As a result, NPL levels may be understated and not directly comparable.

Moreover, central banks and statistical authorities typically only report NPL levels at banks, not considering NPLs potentially warehoused at AMCs or in special purpose vehicle structures, usually set up as related parties, to clean up banks' balance sheets.

Table 3 summarizes NPL classification methodologies adopted in the countries studied.

Table 3: Summary of Nonperforming Loan Classification Methodologies Adopted in Studied Countries

Country	IFRS 9/Local Equivalent Compliance	Date of Adoption	NPL reporting	Basis for Provision	Comments
People's Republic of China	IFRS 9 compliant	1 January 2018	Over 90 days past due including substandard, doubtful and loss loans	Expected loss	Loans are classified into five categories (pass, special mention, substandard, doubtful, and loss) based on a set of qualitative and quantitative factors. NPLs are defined as loans with over 90 days past due including substandard, doubtful and loss loans.
Indonesia	Indonesia financial accounting standards–PSAK 71–IFRS 9 compliant	1 January 2020	Over 90 days past due including substandard (90–120 days past due), doubtful (120–180 days past due), and loss (over 180 days past due)	Expected loss	PSAK 71 is consistent with IFRS 9 in all significant aspects, i.e., the recognition of expected credit loss and appropriate staging classification of the loan exposure. The latest available official NPL statistics from the Bank of Indonesia continue to be defined as over 90 days past due. Before 2020, the central bank ordered the special provisions (after collateral value has been deducted) to be: • substandard – 15% • doubtful – 50% • loss – 100%
Kazakhstan	IFRS 9 compliant	1 January 2018	Over 90 days past due	Expected loss	Notwithstanding IFRS 9 adoption, official NPL statistics from the National Bank of Kazakhstan continue to be based on (and limited to) loans with over 90 days past due. Financial institutions also report loans by stages in their financial statements. The central bank also shows NPL coverage based on 90 days past due and overall impairment allowance.
Republic of Korea	Korean version of IFRS–KIFRS 1109–IFRS 9 compliant	1 January 2018	Over 90 days past due including substandard, doubtful, and estimated loss loans.	Expected loss	Loans are classified into five categories (normal, precautionary, substandard, doubtful, and estimated loss) based on a set of qualitative and quantitative factors. NPL is defined as loans with over 90 days past due including substandard, doubtful, and estimated loss loans. NPLs are presented as "substandard and below loans" in banks' annual reports.
Malaysia	MFRS 9 - IFRS 9 compliant	1 January 2018	Stage 3 loans	Expected loss	According to the Malaysian Accounting Standard Board, MFRS 9 is equivalent to IFRS 9 Financial Instruments; entities that comply with MFRS 9 will simultaneously be compliant with IFRS 9.

continued on next page

Table 3 *continued*

Country	IFRS 9/Local Equivalent Compliance	Date of Adoption	NPL reporting	Basis for Provision	Comments
Thailand	Thai Financial Reporting Standard 9–IFRS 9 compliant	1 January 2020	Stage 3 loans	Expected loss	Before 2020, loans were classified into six categories (pass, special mention, substandard, doubtful, doubtful of loss, and loss) based on a set of qualitative and quantitative factors determined by banks in accordance with the Bank of Thailand regulations and guidelines. NPLs were defined as loans with over 90 days past due (substandard, doubtful, doubtful of loss, and loss), which required a provision of 100% for the difference between gross book value and present value of expected cash flows from repayments or sales of collateral. Loss loans shall be written off.
Viet Nam	Has not adopted IFRS 9	Proposed 2025	Over 90 days past due including substandard (91-180 days past due), doubtful (181-360 days past due), and loss (over 360 days past due)	Incurred loss	Specific provision requirements for NPLs as percentage of balance (deducting the value of any security assets): • substandard – 20% • doubtful – 50% • loss – 100% Viet Nam Financial Reporting Standards were approved by the Ministry of Finance in March 2020, requiring all enterprises to adopt the new standard from 2025. This currently excludes credit institutions, and a separate agenda is yet to be announced by the State Bank of Viet Nam.

IFRS = International Financial Reporting Standards, KIFRS = Korean International Financial Reporting Standards, MFRS = Malaysia Financial Reporting Standards, NPL = nonperforming loan, PSAK = Indonesian Financial Accounting Standards.

Source: Deloitte research based on public information.

Potential Future Trends

According to the International Monetary Fund and central bank data, NPLs held by banking institutions across selected economies in Asia and the Pacific amounted to over $794 billion by the end of 2021, up from $766 billion in 2020 and $692 billion in 2019. East Asia and the PRC account for over half of the total stock (71.2%), and the rest arises mainly from South Asia (15.5%) and Southeast Asia (9.3%) (Figure 1).

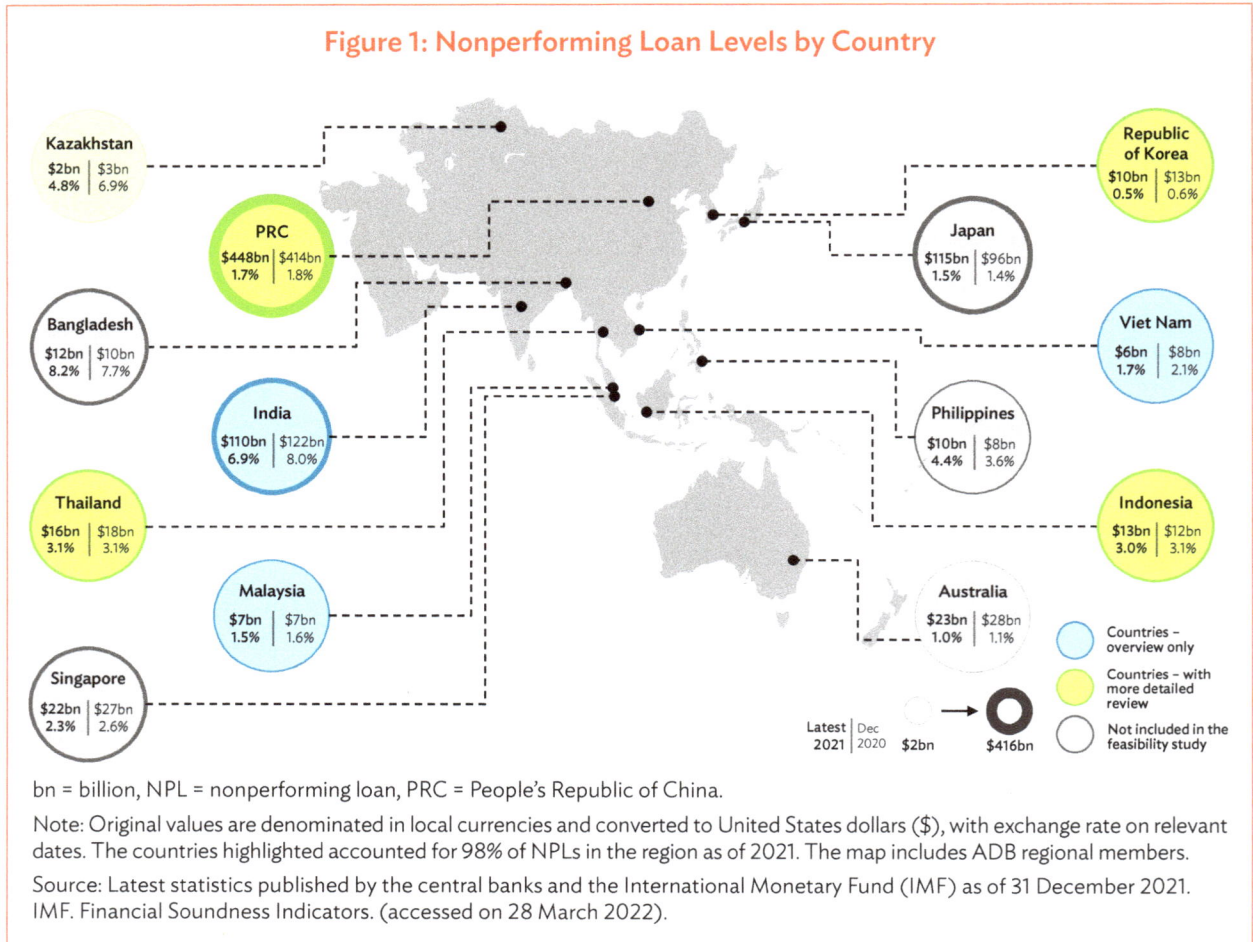

Figure 1: Nonperforming Loan Levels by Country

Country	Latest 2021	Dec 2020
Kazakhstan	$2bn / 4.8%	$3bn / 6.9%
PRC	$448bn / 1.7%	$414bn / 1.8%
Bangladesh	$12bn / 8.2%	$10bn / 7.7%
India	$110bn / 6.9%	$122bn / 8.0%
Thailand	$16bn / 3.1%	$18bn / 3.1%
Malaysia	$7bn / 1.5%	$7bn / 1.6%
Singapore	$22bn / 2.3%	$27bn / 2.6%
Republic of Korea	$10bn / 0.5%	$13bn / 0.6%
Japan	$115bn / 1.5%	$96bn / 1.4%
Viet Nam	$6bn / 1.7%	$8bn / 2.1%
Philippines	$10bn / 4.4%	$8bn / 3.6%
Indonesia	$13bn / 3.0%	$12bn / 3.1%
Australia	$23bn / 1.0%	$28bn / 1.1%

Legend:
- Countries – overview only
- Countries – with more detailed review
- Not included in the feasibility study

bn = billion, NPL = nonperforming loan, PRC = People's Republic of China.

Note: Original values are denominated in local currencies and converted to United States dollars ($), with exchange rate on relevant dates. The countries highlighted accounted for 98% of NPLs in the region as of 2021. The map includes ADB regional members.

Source: Latest statistics published by the central banks and the International Monetary Fund (IMF) as of 31 December 2021. IMF. Financial Soundness Indicators. (accessed on 28 March 2022).

While the full extent of increases in NPLs may not be known for some time and forecasts may be updated, Moody's (the credit rating agency), in October 2020, forecast NPLs to double on average across 14 key economies in Asia and the Pacific by 2022 (Australia; Bangladesh; the PRC; Hong Kong, China; India; Indonesia; Japan; the Republic of Korea; Malaysia; Philippines; Singapore; Sri Lanka; Thailand; and Viet Nam), as COVID-19 relief measures are unwound, such as regulatory forbearances.

As part of the preparations of this report, seven public AMCs in the region were surveyed covering five countries, considering the potential impact of the COVID-19 pandemic on NPL levels.[1] Respondents from most countries

---

[1]   Please refer to the Appendix on p. 51 for a list of interviewed and surveyed partner institutions during the preparations of this report.

were expecting NPL stock to increase slightly from current levels and peak in 2021 and, in certain countries, to increase more than 1.5 times the current levels by 2022. Increases are expected to mostly come from corporate, small and medium-sized enterprises (SMEs) lending (especially tourism sector loans), commercial real estate, credit card and/or unsecured personal loans, and unsecured business loans.

Nonperforming Loan Resolution Practices and the Role of Asset Management Companies

AMCs have been fundamental to NPL resolution in the region since the Asian financial crisis in the late 1990s. AMCs typically hold and manage nonperforming assets removed from the balance sheets of credit institutions as a tool to improve the asset quality of the financial system. Most AMCs aim to maximize the recovery value of distressed assets, while some function simply as a warehouse of NPLs with minimal collection activities.

In many countries in the region, licensed national or regional AMCs are the sole means by which banks can dispose of their NPL portfolios, with AMCs thereafter assuming responsibility for ongoing management and disposal.

Special purpose vehicle structures are increasingly being used to warehouse problem loans and restore bank balance sheets. Several Indonesian banks, for example, have set up special purpose vehicles to warehouse and workout their NPLs to improve their balance sheets. However, in most cases, the originating banks continue to service these NPLs. Similar measures have been taken in other countries, including Kazakhstan; although, warehousing on its own will not resolve high underlying NPL levels.

Based on survey results and discussions with study participants (footnote 1), workout and restructuring remain the most common methods banks and AMCs adopt for NPL resolution, including write-off, deferrals, and debt restructuring, as well as formal court enforcement and insolvency processes.

In this respect, since the global financial crisis, governments and regulators have taken significant steps to improve overall operation of the courts to tackle (in many cases) significant backlogs, resolving inconsistencies, and simplifying enforcement and recovery processes. In Indonesia, for instance, overall insolvency and the restructuring framework have significantly improved, according to the World Bank's Doing Business, Resolving Insolvency Survey of 2015 and 2019 (Table 4), including enforcement time and recovery rates.

Table 4: World Bank—Insolvency Regime Effectiveness

Location	Rank		Score		Recovery Rate (cents on $)		Time (years)		Cost (% of estate)		Outcome[a]	Strength of Insolvency Framework Index (0–16)	
	2019	2015	2019	2015	2019	2015	2019	2015	2019	2015		2019	2015
PRC	51	53	62.1	55.3	36.9	36.0	1.7	1.7	22.0	22.0	0	13.5	11.5
Indonesia	38	75	68.1	46.8	65.5	31.7	1.1	1.9	21.6	22.0	1	10.5	9.5
Kazakhstan	42	63	66.7	51.5	39.8	43.5	1.5	1.5	15.0	15.0	0	14.5	9.0
Korea, Rep. of	11	5	82.9	90.1	84.3	83.1	1.5	1.5	3.5	4.0	1	12.0	14.5
Malaysia	40	36	67.0	65.6	81.0	81.3	1.0	1.0	10.0	10.0	1	7.5	7.0
Thailand	24	45	76.8	58.7	70.1	42.3	1.5	2.7	18.0	36.0	1	12.5	11.5
Viet Nam	122	104	38.0	41.3	21.3	18.6	5.0	5.0	14.5	15.0	0	8.5	10.0

PRC = People's Republic of China; Korea, Rep. of = Republic of Korea.
[a] 0 as piecemeal sale and 1 as going concern.
Source: World Bank. 2015 and 2019. Doing Business—Resolving Insolvency.

Table 4 looks at insolvency regimes in studied countries. As noted, the majority improved their rankings between 2015 and 2019. In Viet Nam, the average duration of proceedings remains quite long (5 years) and recovery rates low. In the PRC, recovery rates are, comparatively, generally low and costs high.

Nonperforming Loan Market Activity

It is difficult to generalize NPL market activity for a market as large and diverse as developing Asia.

Direct sales

The PRC's NPL market is the largest and most active, with an NPL stock of CNY2.7 trillion ($414 billion) at the end of 2020 (CIBRC 2021) and had increased to $448 billion by the end of 2021. The total outstanding principal balance of NPLs sold in primary and secondary markets reached CNY859 billion ($125 billion) in 2019 (with primary market estimated at $65 billion and secondary at $60 billion), of which about 80% or CNY681 billion ($105 billion) are portfolio transactions.[2] NPL disposals reduced in 2020 to CNY714 billion ($103 billion), of which around 48% were primary trades. The relative rates of primary and secondary trades and the impact of the unwinding of the COVID-19 relief measures suggest that the overall stocks of NPLs are likely to continue to rise in the coming years.

In the PRC, banks can only sell loan portfolios (with over two connections) to licensed national and provincial AMCs, which may thereafter act as intermediaries for sales to investors. Historically, most such sales have been to domestic investors—in 2019 only 2% was sold to investors outside mainland PRC. Moreover, until recently, personal loans could not be transferred other than on a single name basis. However, the People's Bank of China, in January 2021, initiated a pilot programme and the first ever portfolio trade of personal loans was completed in early March 2021.

As in the PRC, the NPL secondary market in the Republic of Korea may also be considered mature, with NPL sales of $3.5 billion in 2020 (about $4 billion in 2019). The main buyers in the country are privately owned investors, with United Asset Management Company and Daishin Securities being two of the most active. Based on discussions with the Korea Asset Management Corporation, foreign investors are less active these days, reflecting a more mature, lower return market and enough domestic capacity.

In other countries, markets are still developing and publicly available information is limited.

Nonperforming Loan securitizations

The Republic of Korea used NPL securitizations extensively during the Asian financial crisis, but has since reduced them, with levels in 2020 down 6.5% (from 2019) to $2.7 billion (FSS 2021).

The PRC had the highest NPL securitization issuance in 2020, at $4.3 billion, with 60% of deals completed in the fourth quarter (Bloomberg China 2020).

Elsewhere, while NPL securitization frameworks exist, they have not been used much in recent years. In Malaysia, for instance, the first NPL securitization was originated by AmBank in 2007 via two offerings for a combined RM240.8 million ($70.9 million); however, the NPL securitization market has not been particularly active since. The reasons for low securitizations are unclear; the limited guidance available from the regulator in certain jurisdictions creates legal uncertainty, which may deter new securitizations.

---

[2]   Public announcements for transactions. For example, see: Economic Daily. 2018. The Shenzhen Branch of China Great Wall Asset Management Co., Ltd. Plans to Dispose of the Creditor's Rights of 8 Enterprises Including Anke Robot Co., Ltd. Public Announcement. 29 November.

Table 5 summarizes secondary NPL markets for the Asian countries studied.

Table 5: Summary of Nonperforming Loan Secondary Market for Studied Countries in Asia

Country	Direct NPL Sales	NPL Securitizations
PRC	• Banks can only sell loan portfolios (with over two connections) to licensed national and provincial AMCs. • However, an AMC licence is not required when purchasing portfolios from AMCs or acquiring single positions (regardless of source). • Personal loans cannot be transferred in the form of portfolios; a pilot programme was launched in January 2021 to allow participating banks to sell portfolios of personal loans (excluding mortgages and auto loans) to eligible AMCs. • Based on public data, the total outstanding principal balance of NPL transactions in 2019 reached **CNY859 billion ($125 billion)**—CNY443 billion ($65 billion) in the primary market (from banks to AMCs and other entities), and CNY416 billion ($60 billion) in the secondary market. • NPLs acquired by investors based outside of mainland PRC only comprise 2% of the CNY416 billion sold via the secondary market in 2019. • As reported by Zheshang AMC, **CNY714 billion ($103 billion) of NPLs were transacted in 2020**. The primary market saw 48% of the total volume (or CNY343 billion).	• According to Bloomberg China, the total issuance of securitization products backed by NPLs was CNY28.1 billion ($4.3 billion) in 2020, the highest since the approval of the NPL securitization pilot programme in 2016; 60% of the issuance was completed in the fourth quarter of 2020. • Nevertheless, this is a fraction of the overall amount of NPLs traded on the secondary market.
Indonesia	• There have been several successful deals completed recently. Bank Permata, HSBC, CIMB Niaga (as sellers) disposed of their portfolios, primarily corporate/SME loans backed by real estate properties, to buyers including several foreign investors (e.g., Macquarie Capital, CarVal, and DW Capital). • The aggregate size of NPL transactions is not available due to limited disclosures.	• The Financial Services Authority has issued regulations concerning securitization. There is no specific guidance on NPL securitization. • We have not yet noted any NPL securitization structures in the market.
Kazakhstan	• The Problem Loans Fund is the main buyer for NPLs in Kazakhstan. It disclosed that it had concluded its most recent NPL purchase in 2019. The fund acquired a portfolio of agricultural loans for T640 billion ($1.6 billion). Since incorporation, the fund has acquired T3,794 billion (about $11.4 billion) of problem loans from multiple local banks. • In 2019, the fund sold T12.7 billion worth of assets through the web portal of the State Property Register (the single operator of this platform is JSC Information Accounting Centre), all to domestic buyers. On its corporate website, the fund advertises the sale of property for marketing purposes.	• The governing framework for securitization transactions does not have specific provisions around NPL securitization. • The market has not observed any NPL securitizations since the global financial crisis.

continued on next page

Table 5 *continued*

Country	Direct NPL Sales	NPL Securitizations
	• However, banks and other NPL holders can sell assets on the market through their own websites. Total NPL transactions by other entities in the market have not been tracked and are therefore not publicly available.	
Republic of Korea	• Considered to have one of the most developed secondary markets for NPLs. • According to a related industry source quoted in the local capital market media (The Bell), **the NPL sale volume in 2020 was W3.75 trillion ($3.5 billion)**, down W600 billion ($540 million) from 2019. • Apart from selling to KAMCO, a large portion of the NPLs were transferred to private sector investors including United Asset Management Corporation, which has become a significant player in the market.	• The first NPL securitization was launched by KAMCO in 1999. • According to the Financial Supervisory Service, **total issuance of securitization backed by NPL by banks in 2020 was W2.9 trillion ($2.7 billion)**, a decrease of 6.5% from 2019.
Malaysia	• The market is not particularly active. Historically, there has been a steady stream of small-scale disposals of legacy unsecured stock held by banks. Most of the underlying exposures have already been written off. • A notable secured portfolio transaction was Aiqon Capital's acquisition of the retail and commercial book sold by AmBank. The RM554 million transaction ($134 million, about 10% of face value) was separated into two subportfolios consisting of Islamic and conventional financings.	• AmBank originated the first NPL securitization in 2007 via two offerings for a combined RM240.8 million ($70.9 million). • The NPL securitization market has not been particularly active since.
Thailand	• Large banks have regularly sold portfolios of loans in recent years. • The buyer landscape is dominated by the top two AMCs with nationwide reach—Bangkok Commercial Asset Management and Sukhumvit Asset Management. International investors are also active in the market. • NPL transaction volume data is not publicly available.	• The NPL securitization market has not been active in recent years. • In 2002, SG Asia Credit Securities launched the first rated securitization of distressed assets in Thailand, with a total issuance of B7 billion ($170 million).
Viet Nam	• As reported, Viet Nam Asset Management Company purchased D15 trillion ($662 million) of NPLs with special bonds in 2020. As of December 2020, the total acquisition of bad debts by the company accumulated to D373 trillion ($16.3 billion). The vast majority are warehoused at the Viet Nam Asset Management Company, with the selling banks continuing loan servicing activity. • The transaction volume of NPLs purchased by other entities (such as debt trading companies and AMCs set up by the banks) is not disclosed to the public. Over 50 such companies operated as at the end of 2020, all locally incorporated.	• To date, the regulator has not provided regulations or guidance on the securitization of loans. No NPL-backed securities have been issued in Viet Nam so far.

AMC = asset management company, B = Thai baht, CNY = Chinese yuan, D = Vietnamese dong, KAMCO = Korea Asset Management Corporation, NPL = nonperforming loan, PRC = People's Republic of China, RM = Malaysian ringgit, T = Kazakhstani tenge, W = Korean won.

Source: Authors' compilation based on public information and asset management company inputs.

Overview of Existing Online Trading Platforms Used in the Region

Collateral auction platforms for foreclosed assets already exist in several jurisdictions in Asia (PRC, the Republic of Korea, Kazakhstan) although use of these for NPL secondary trading is still relatively limited (Box 1).

Box 1: Case Study—People's Republic of China

Compared to other countries in the region, the People's Republic of China (PRC) may be considered relatively advanced in terms of bringing nonperforming loan (NPL) disposals online,[a] with Taobao (part of the Alibaba Group) becoming the first online platform for NPL disposal in the country in 2012. In 2016, the Supreme People's Court of the PRC licensed five platforms (Taobao.com, JD.com, People's Court Litigation Asset, Gongpai.com, and Zhongpai) as judicial auction online service providers. In 2019, it licensed another two (Industrial and Commercial Bank of China's Rong E-Gou, and China Beijing Equity Exchange). The table illustrates how the market is structured in the PRC, with asset management companies (AMCs) acting as intermediary between selling banks and investors.

Market Structure

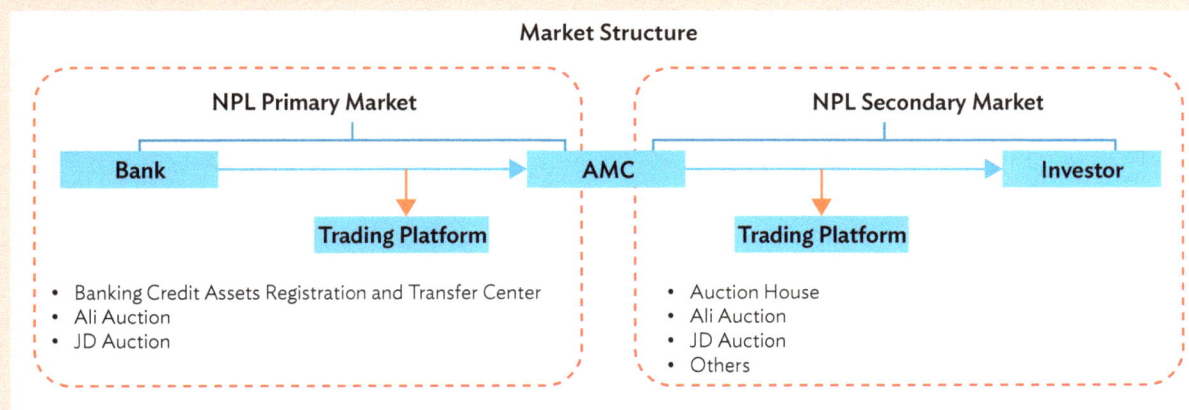

There are many nonperforming assets trading platforms in the PRC, but no uniform national NPL trading platform.

- Licensed AMCs are required to conduct transactions on the designated platforms.
- Private-owned companies and foreign capital are allowed to conduct transactions through negotiated transfer.
- As part of Taobao.com, Ali Auction is also owned by Alibaba Group. Taobao.com is a major player in the Chinese e-commerce market. Ali Auction is one of the leading online auction platforms in the PRC, with transaction volumes of $80 billion (in 2018). Almost all Chinese courts have registered on its judicial sales platform.
- JD Auction is part of JD.com. JD.com, Inc (also known as Jingdong) is a Chinese e-commerce company. As a member of the Fortune Global 500, it is one of the two massive business-to-consumer online retailers in the PRC by transaction volume and revenue.
- Gongpai.com is a public platform of information release and assets auction, which is built by Shanghai Association of Auctioneers. It provides services covering online auction, industry management, and government supervision.
- People's Court Litigation Assets is a specialized public judicial auction platform established and registered by the Supreme People's Court of the PRC. It plays an important leading role in promoting Chinese judicial auction reform.
- 360PAI is an online NPL auction platform developed by Shanghai Baichang Internet Auction Technology Co. Ltd. 360PAI gathered thousands of licensed Chinese auction houses. Although it is not one of the transaction platforms nominated by the Supreme People's Court of the PRC, it is still a popular platform in the PRC NPL industry.

Types of Trading Platform

There are three main types of NPL trading platform: auction house, officially licensed online platform, and other online platforms.

continued on next page

Box 1 *continued*

Feature	Auction House	Officially Licensed Online Platform	Other Online Platforms
Qualification	Auction business license	Cooperation with court	Auction business license
Platform Function	Offline	Online	Online
	Traditional display	Webpage display	Webpage display
	Traditional auction service	Online auction and data service	Online auction and data service
Commission	≤5% of non-art items	5% of transaction price, (2% of the premium in the concessionary period) (Ali auction)	1% of transaction price from both buyer and seller

---

[a] The Republic of Korea also has experience in the field; usage is primarily limited to the auction of assets seized by tax authorities.

Sources: Deloitte research based on public information/ Zheshang Asset Management Company.

While collateral auction platforms for foreclosed assets already exist, the use of these for NPL secondary trading is less prevalent. Figure 2 sets out a range of functionalities, which may be offered through NPL online platforms.

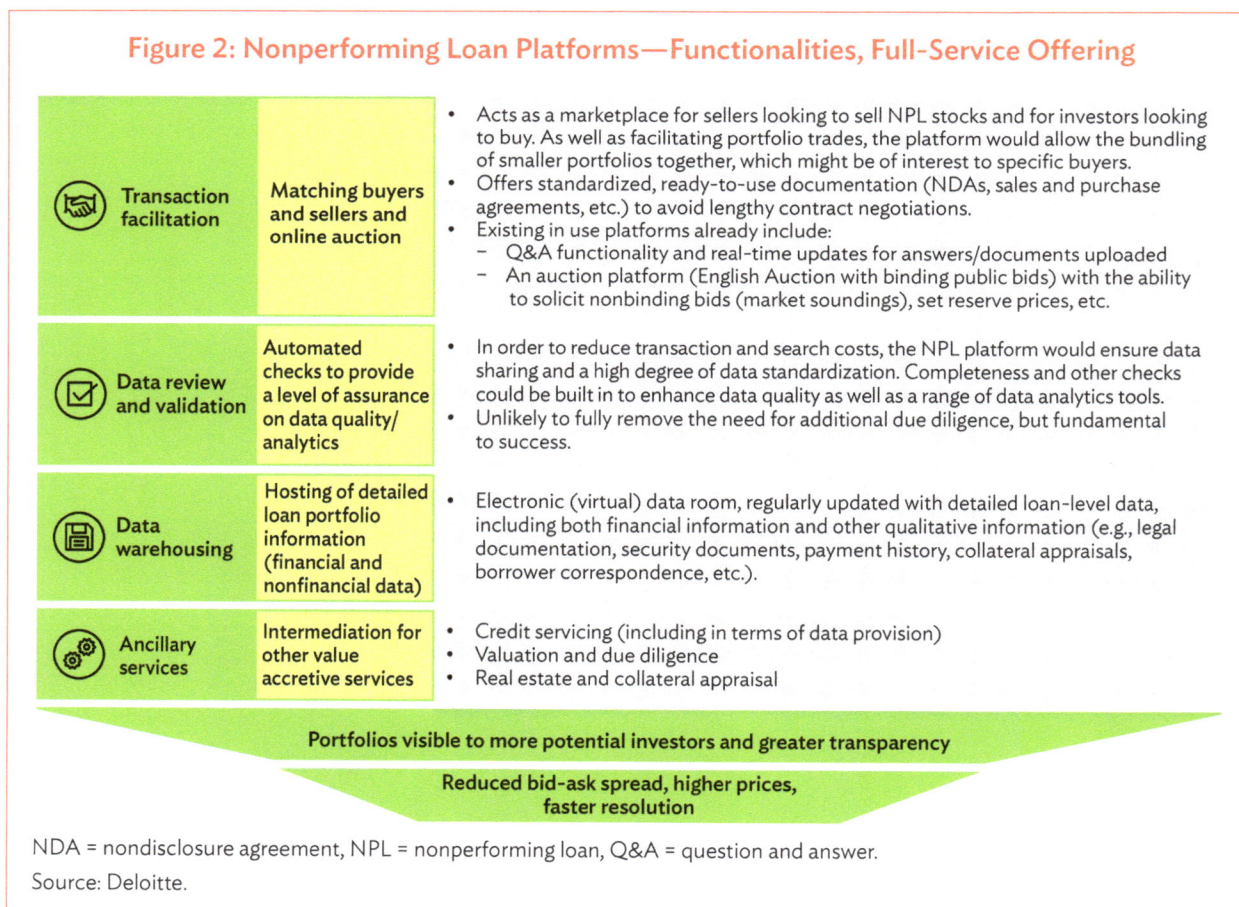

Figure 2: Nonperforming Loan Platforms—Functionalities, Full-Service Offering

Transaction facilitation	Matching buyers and sellers and online auction	• Acts as a marketplace for sellers looking to sell NPL stocks and for investors looking to buy. As well as facilitating portfolio trades, the platform would allow the bundling of smaller portfolios together, which might be of interest to specific buyers.
		• Offers standardized, ready-to-use documentation (NDAs, sales and purchase agreements, etc.) to avoid lengthy contract negotiations.
		• Existing in use platforms already include:
		  – Q&A functionality and real-time updates for answers/documents uploaded
		  – An auction platform (English Auction with binding public bids) with the ability to solicit nonbinding bids (market soundings), set reserve prices, etc.

Data review and validation	Automated checks to provide a level of assurance on data quality/ analytics	• In order to reduce transaction and search costs, the NPL platform would ensure data sharing and a high degree of data standardization. Completeness and other checks could be built in to enhance data quality as well as a range of data analytics tools. • Unlikely to fully remove the need for additional due diligence, but fundamental to success.
Data warehousing	Hosting of detailed loan portfolio information (financial and nonfinancial data)	• Electronic (virtual) data room, regularly updated with detailed loan-level data, including both financial information and other qualitative information (e.g., legal documentation, security documents, payment history, collateral appraisals, borrower correspondence, etc.).
Ancillary services	Intermediation for other value accretive services	• Credit servicing (including in terms of data provision) • Valuation and due diligence • Real estate and collateral appraisal

Portfolios visible to more potential investors and greater transparency

Reduced bid-ask spread, higher prices, faster resolution

NDA = nondisclosure agreement, NPL = nonperforming loan, Q&A = question and answer.
Source: Deloitte.

By contrast, in Asia, typical functionalities are primarily around sale notification, bidding, and auction (including collateral auction), with remaining aspects including due diligence and document hosting mostly dealt with offline (Figure 3).

Figure 3: Typical Online Trading Platform Process

Step 1
The seller publishes notice on the auction.

Step 2 (offline):
Bidders conduct site visit and due diligence.

Step 3
Bidders pay deposits.

Step 4
Bidders submit the bids.

Step 5
The system confirms the winning bidder.

Step 6 (offline):
The buyer and the seller close the transfer offline.

Source: Authors' compilation based on Taobao process.

Step 1—The seller publishes an online notice including a basic description of the asset, any defects, key documentation, seller's reserve price, eligibility of the bidders, auction process, timeline, contact details of the seller, etc.

Step 2—Based on the (nonconfidential) information provided in the public notice, interested buyers proceed with due diligence, which may be managed offline. All information provided on the main auction page will be fully public and will not require a nondisclosure agreement (NDA). While some platforms offer data warehousing or virtual data room functionalities for NPLs (e.g., Debitos in Europe), not all platforms do this. In such a scenario, further details would be obtained from the seller or the seller's agent and NDAs might be required.

Step 3—To participate in the auction, bidders may need to pay a deposit through the platform's online payment system. The deposit will be frozen until the end of the bidding process.

Step 4—Once the deposit is paid, a bidder can submit their bid on the auction page. All bids submitted are live, anonymized, and visible to other participants. Bidders can also increase their bids during the bidding period. By way of example, the Taobao platform suggests 12 hours for movable assets and 24 hours for immovable assets. However, the seller has the option to change the bidding period to suit the nature of the assets and participants (e.g., if based in different time zones).

Step 5—The highest bidder wins the auction, and the system automatically generates a confirmation letter stating the winning bidder. Where the sale is by way of judicial auction, (e.g., in the PRC), the confirmation letter is published on the auction page, stating the name of the vendor, the buyer, and transacted price—thus providing full transparency. For other (nonjudicial) auctions, including NPL sales by banks or AMCs, details will not be made fully public. The confirmation letter will be used as a supporting document to complete the signing and closing process. The successful bidder thereafter remits the outstanding amount (less deposit already paid) to a bank account specified by the seller or completes the payment through the platform's online portal.

Step 6—The buyer contacts the seller offline to execute the transaction documentation and complete the transfer.

Both loans and collateralized assets may be traded, dependent on jurisdiction. Typical asset classes offered on the platforms are presented in Table 6.

Table 6: Asset Classes Traded on Online Platforms in Asia

Asset Classes	Specific Assets
Immovable assets	• Land use rights/forest use rights/sea use rights/mining rights • Real estate properties • Construction in progress
Movable assets	• Automobiles • Vessels • Equipment and machinery • Inventories • Luxury goods
Financial assets	• Nonperforming loans • Shares • Account receivables
Other intangible assets	• Intellectual property (copyrights, patents, trademarks, etc.)

Source: Authors' compilation.

Ancillary services may also be provided through the platforms, as follows.

Noticeboard. Sellers can also use the platform as a notice board to market assets. The seller fills in a simple teaser (a suggested format may be provided), which can be viewed by the general public. Interested parties contact the seller online or using the contact details provided in the teaser.

Cooperation with third parties. The platform acts as an intermediary between investors and third-party advisors, providing services such as asset appraisal, legal advisory, due diligence and execution support, tax advisory, etc.

Cloud-based advisory services. Leveraging their database of transactions, platforms may provide the following advisory services to sellers:

- Asset pricing (for real estate properties and automobiles): Sellers have the option to use the online pricing services provided by the platform. The valuation is conducted using the comparable pricing method based on past transactions of similar assets. Considering its simplicity, some courts encourage the use of online asset pricing as benchmarks for reserve prices in order to facilitate the judicial auction processes.
- Targeted marketing (Taobao 2021): The platform maintains a database of investors with their investment needs and appetites. If the seller chooses to use the targeted marketing services, the platform will shortlist suitable investors by matching investment criteria with characteristics of the asset and communicate with the potential investors to determine interest.

The benefits of NPL online platforms are discussed in Chapter II, along with other prerequisites considered for the development of deeper secondary markets.

II. Methodological Approach

The economic impact of high NPLs on the banking system and the broader economy has been well documented (Lee and Rosenkranz 2019; Park and Shin 2020; Huljak et al. 2020). High NPL ratios may increase banks' capital requirements and funding costs, reduce bank profits, and brake further lending in the real economy, tying up other scare resources, including human capital. As set out in recent research by the European Central Bank, high and unresolved NPLs are also associated with deeper recessions and slower recoveries (ECB 2020).

Against this background, well-developed secondary markets for NPLs have multiple benefits for banks, which face high stocks of NPLs and seek to engage in active NPL portfolio sale strategies to clean up their balance sheets and generate external capital. For central banks, regulators, and policy makers, they promote financial stability and help manage macrofinancial risk.

Growth in NPL secondary markets, while maintaining a high borrower protection, would substantially support collective efforts to tackle the potential upcoming flows of impaired loans. As noted, while the full extent of the increase may not be known for some time and estimates may change, in October 2020, Moody's forecast that NPLs in the Asia and Pacific region could double by the end of 2022 as COVID-19 relief measures unwound, albeit at differing rates across the region. Updated forecasts of NPL ratios and recoveries after COVID-19 as of November 2020 indicated that the PRC's NPL ratio would increase from 1.9% in 2019 to 5.6% (COVID-19 maximum based on macro scenarios from the International Monetary Fund) and for the Republic of Korea from 0.3% to 2.6% (Heppe 2020).

When liquid secondary markets are present, different tools are available for banks to address NPLs—for example, by direct sales by banks to outside investors (possibly in parallel to a recapitalization of the bank); securitization, possibly involving asset protection schemes; and use of AMCs. Moreover, access to a functioning secondary market in Asia could provide benefits beyond NPLs, including sales of noncore assets.

Furthermore, foreign participants in the domestic NPL markets may offer banks access to larger capital pools, which can absorb more bad debts. When combined with a well-developed independent loan servicing industry, the potential moral hazard issue can also be ameliorated, as the risk exposures are transferred and managed by third-party specialists instead of the originating banks.

Against this background, online auction platforms have significant potential to broaden the channels for NPL disposal, help mitigate information asymmetry, and break down geographical boundaries.

The rest of this chapter considers in more detail the benefits of online NPL platforms in further developing markets; the NPL transaction lifecycle and how this can be adapted to online trading; and the prerequisites for a functioning NPL market, featuring narrowed bid-ask spreads, a broad pool of investors, and capacity for cross-border trades.

A.   Potential Benefits of Online Nonperforming Loan Platforms

Compared to other disposal processes, online NPL transaction platforms offer potentially significant process benefits to users including:

- wider and deeper channels to market, and better matching between buyers and sellers;
- faster execution (anecdotally, existing platform operators talk about between 55% and 90% reduction in times compared to offline processes);
- lower transaction costs; and
- better pricing compared to offline disposals.

For AMCs, these factors would be of considerable benefit in addressing potential liquidity issues, which (as participants in this study commented) represent a limiting factor in pursuing their financial stability mandate.

The pandemic, and its related lockdown measures to slow the spread of the disease, has had a profound impact on how people work and interact. The internet has allowed businesses to adapt new solutions at speed in a way unthought of previously.

Various studies have noted the acceleration of digital adoptions at both organizational and industry levels between 2017 and 2019 (McKinsey & Company 2020). Digital platforms are transforming how people work. With such platforms, new business models have proliferated, offering enormous economic potential (ADB 2021b).

Considering overall market resilience, transaction platforms have the potential to facilitate and maintain active, liquid, and efficient secondary markets, in the same way as digital warehouses have for consumer goods during the lockdown. As an online marketplace, which can be accessed remotely through secure internet channels with all necessary documentation digitized, these online transaction platforms would be able to continue to function on a largely uninterrupted basis.

Discussions with the United States (US) platform operators, as part of this study, suggested that, whereas European and other markets may have been stymied as a result of the pandemic, secure technology and online platforms have enabled them to continue transacting sales as usual. They also suggested that, based on the volume handled in 2020, sales in the US held steady and, in certain circumstances, increased as some banking clients took advantage of strong pricing out of concern for future increases in NPLs.[3] Government-sponsored enterprises (Fannie Mae and Freddie Mac) did not have as many NPL sales in 2020 as 2019, but this was because of ongoing deferrals, foreclosure moratoria, and government stimulus and concerns on how those issues might affect pricing by investors.

As noted in Figure 4, NPL transaction volumes in Europe and Asia were significantly lower in 2020 because of the pandemic; however, the drop is less in the PRC (about 17%) than in Europe (about 53%). While this may, in large part, reflect more effective containment measures and a faster return to business as usual, the availability of existing online platforms may have had the same effect as suggested by US commentators in allowing the market to keep functioning.

---

[3]   NPL transaction data in the US is not readily available, with no registry or database that collects the information, mainly because the trades are confidential for the most part; accordingly, these comments remain largely anecdotal.

Figure 4: Nonperforming Loan Transaction Volumes, Europe, and the People's Republic of China, 2018–2020 Comparison
($ billion)

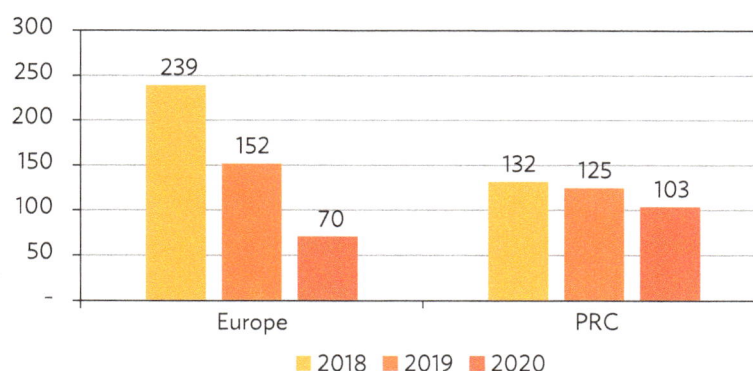

PRC = People's Republic of China.

Note: For Europe, data include the following countries: Austria, Bosnia and Herzegovina, Bulgaria, Croatia, Cyprus, Czech Republic, Denmark, Estonia, Finland, France, Germany, Greece, Hungary, Iceland, Ireland, Italy, Lithuania, Netherlands, Norway, Poland, Portugal, Romania, Serbia, Slovenia, Spain, Sweden, United Kingdom, and Ukraine.

Sources: Transaction announcements (as the second quarter 2021); Debtwire; and Zheshang Asset Management Company.

A wide range of loans could be made available on platforms (asset focus is discussed in Chapter V), costs could be shared and reduced, the scope of participants could be broadened beyond the domestic sector, and services from across countries could be provided through the platforms.

NPL online platforms would contribute to reducing the degree of market dysfunction in markets for NPLs, helping to address information asymmetries, increase creditor coordination, and broaden the investor base, thus improving market pricing of NPLs.

B.   Nonperforming Loan Transaction Lifecycle

Consideration of the NPL transaction lifecycle helps show how the process might be moved online and the potential challenges. In broad terms, four main phases can be seen.

Phase 1-Sales Planning and Phase 2-Preparation include defining the sales strategy and setting the transaction perimeter as well as initial vendor due diligence, legal due diligence (including around transferability), document extraction, and data room preparation. Depending on the nature of the portfolio, this may take several months to complete and include significant heavy lifting in document extraction.

Phase 3-Transaction Execution could be split into one or two stages, typically lasting 6–8 weeks in total (however, it could be longer for sizable portfolios or where there are document extraction issues), following initial information disclosure, and may include the option for nonbinding bids so as to sift the buyer population to focus effort and highlight potential expectation gaps.

Bidding may be either open and visible to all parties or sealed (other bidders cannot see what is being offered), with different schools of thought as to which provides the best price execution. Sealed bid auctions are used where there is likely significant interest in an asset and the market is strong and is a way for sellers to receive multiple bids before settling on a final price, with a chance that they get a better price. Open bids offer greater transparency and may therefore be more common in developing markets, where building confidence in the process is important.

Phase 4-Transaction Closing follows offer acceptance and includes detailed contract negotiation (based on draft documents, which typically are circulated earlier in the process), including over any representations, warranties, and settlement. This would take place on a bilateral basis and is predominantly done offline.

Figure 5 shows the typical NPL transaction process, from portfolio selection and process design, through to information preparation, notification, due diligence, the auction process, and completion. Some aspects of the process lend themselves more readily to being managed through an online platform (e.g., notification and bidding).

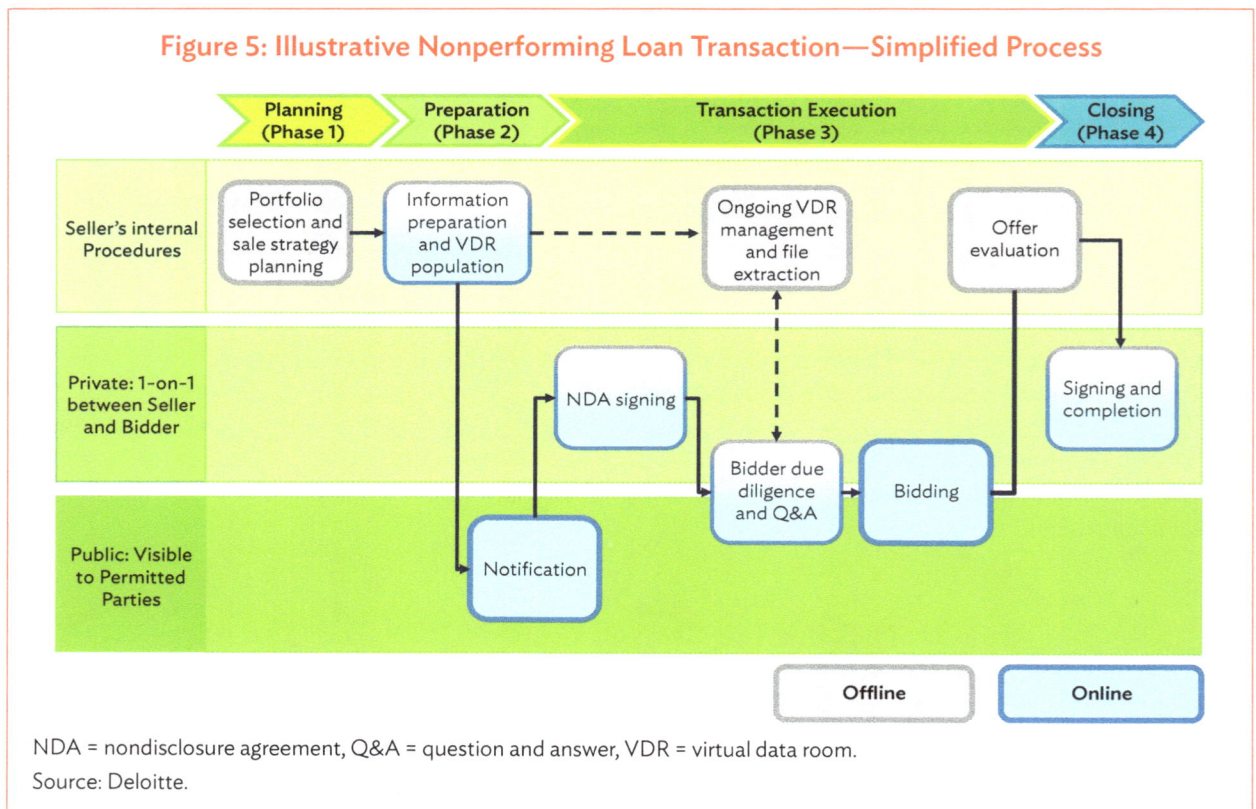

Figure 5: Illustrative Nonperforming Loan Transaction—Simplified Process

NDA = nondisclosure agreement, Q&A = question and answer, VDR = virtual data room.
Source: Deloitte.

Table 7 shows the process from a seller's (or seller's advisor's) perspective, including the different activities as typically observed. Considering the nature of the different activities, many may sensibly migrate to being hosted online to enhance the efficiency of the lifecycle. Moreover, this could be done on a modular basis without necessarily having to move all steps online at the same time. For example, connecting buyers and sellers and distributing an initial teaser could be moved online first, with more extensive document sharing and due diligence following at a later stage.

Table 7: Nonperforming Loan Transaction Lifecycle—Seller's Perspective Illustrative

Sale Preparation	Sale Execution		Deal Negotiation	Post-Sale Activity
Sale Preparation	**Phase I**	**Phase II**	**Deal Negotiation**	**Post-Sale Activity**
Commercial diligence	• NDAs distributed to select investors interested in the portfolio	• Access to a comprehensive electronic dataroom that contains all relevant information including underlying loan documents	• Lead the final SPA negotiations and closing arrangements	**Migration support (if required)**
• VDD/Datatape	• Following information is made available to investors via a dataroom:	• Updated documents (valuation reports, if required) and material correspondence with the borrower are uploaded to the dataroom	• Coordinate with the legal advisor and other advisors on the legal documentations and to resolve open issues	• Migration of obligations as per the SPA, which will include
• Loan and borrower information review	– **Information Memorandum:** Includes details about the portfolio and case summaries for top borrowers in the portfolio	• Updated status for each credit is provided throughout the process (as required)	• Coordinate and support legal advisors with any approvals process	– Electronic system data transfer
• Indicative pricing (for the entire portfolio on a line-by-line basis)	– **Data Tape:** Containing key information on the underlying loan, borrowers, and security; historical payment information, etc.	• Q&A submitted by bidders; turnaround time is generally 2–3 working days	• Signing of SPA	– Physical borrower files transfer
• Collateral valuations, if relevant	– **Limited Q&A:** Questions are generally restricted to clarification on the process and information provided	• Bidders provided with a draft SPA		– Transfer of title in land registry
• Document collection		• Bidders review and submit comments on the SPA		– Transfer of any third-party contracts
• Dataroom management	• Investors submit a nonbinding offer for the Portfolio	• Investors submit binding offers		– Communication to borrowers on sale and transfer of servicing
• Teaser and information memorandum preparation	• Based on the offers received, a limited number of investors proceed to the second phase of the transaction	• Offer evaluation		– Interim servicing and reporting to successful bidder
• Identification of buyers (suitable screening)		• Successful bidder pays deposit		
• Reporting and support				
Legal diligence				
• Identification of diligence requirements				
• Coordination of legal and regulatory diligence				

NDA = nondisclosure agreement, Q&A = question and answer, SPA = sale and purchase agreement, VDD = vendor due diligence.

Source: Deloitte.

Loan Data Tapes and Nonfinancial Data

Fundamental to the process is the loan data tape, drawn from the bank's systems, which will collate all relevant borrower and loan-level information, including around loan exposure and terms, borrower financial performance, security and collateral information, among others. The information typically provided in a data tape is set out in Table 8.

Table 8: Typical Data Tape Fields

Data Tape	Data	Key Fields			
Borrower Tape	Detailed information on the borrower, including borrower name, type of borrower, legal status, jurisdiction, and historical drawdowns	• Borrower ID • Borrower name • Current balance • Updated property market value • Previous property market value	• Original property market value • Borrower industrial classification • Borrower economic sector	• Primary property use • Borrower region/ jurisdiction • Months in arrears • Borrower status	• Weighted average maturity • Weighted average seasoning • Weighted average interest rate • LTV
Loan Tape	Detailed information on the loans, including outstanding balance, interest rate, and interest type	• Loan ID • Borrower ID • Current balance • Currency • Completion date	• Loan term • Maturity date • Seasoning • Amortization type	• Payment frequency • Rate type • Reference rate • Margin	• Gross rate • Undrawn commitment • Whether in receivership
Property Tape (if applicable)	Detailed information on the collateral, including asset type and market value	• Property ID • Borrower ID • Address • Town • District • Region • Postcode • Title numbers	• Property type • Previous market valuation • Date of last valuation • Valuer • Original value • Original valuation date	• Original valuer • Tenure • Year built • Current gross rent • Estimated market rent • Current balance • Net initial yield	• Net equivalent yield • Net reversionary yield • Number of units • Main tenant • Charge • Prior charge amount
Tenancy Tape (if applicable)	Detailed information on the property and subunits, including tenant names and rental values	• Property ID • Borrower ID • Tenancy ID • Tenant name	• Current gross rent • Estimated historic market rent • Lease expiry date	• Adopted passing rent	• Number of units • Estimated forward market rent
Sales Tracker	Detailed information on historic and current asset sale processes				
Guarantor Tape	If loans have guarantees attached, details such as guarantor name, amount, and type are disclosed				
Payment History	Borrower interest and capital payment history	• Borrower ID • Historical capital payments (since origination) • Historical interest payments (since origination)			

ID = identifier, LTV = loan-to-value.
Source: Deloitte.

Additional nonfinancial information will be required for due diligence. Its provision needs to be balanced as this will have an impact on bidders' ability to undertake due diligence. If due diligence is restricted, then enhanced protection may be required by the bidders in the form of representations and warranties.

Bidder diligence and pricing hinge on providing a robust, accurate, and detailed dataset in a timely manner. Delays in document provision and poor-quality information will undermine investor confidence and ultimately result in lower pricing or fewer bids being received. Figure 6 illustrates types of nonfinancial information, which may be required for investor due diligence.

In many cases, documents may have to be manually extracted, cleansed, and catalogued, making for a potentially very labor-intensive process, particularly for large loan portfolios with a significant number of underlying borrowers. Good upfront preparation is, therefore, fundamental to a successful process. Figure 7 shows the approach typically taken to document extraction from a seller's perspective.

Figure 6: Typical Nonperforming Loan Documentation Requirements for Investor Due Diligence

Category	Subcategory	Description
Legal	Facility and security documents	Facility letters, security reviews, guarantees, deeds of security
Legal	Inter-creditor agreements	Deeds of subordination, deeds of priority, duty of care agreements
Legal	Restructuring documents	Settlement agreements, reservation of rights letters, default notices
Legal	Third-party documents	Engagement letters, reports, estimated outcome statements
Legal	Corporate documents	Borrower structure charts, certificates of incorporation, resolutions, articles of association
Legal	Property documents	Leases, sale contracts, litigation documents, title certificates
Commercial	Material correspondence	Acceptance offers, meeting notes, site visit notes
Commercial	Trading data	Financial and management account, business plans, financial projections
Commercial	Credit	Borrower credit files and internal credit papers
Commercial	Performance	Independent business review reports
Commercial	Others	Most recent valuation reports and property insurance documents
Other	Litigation	Details of litigation, correspondence and legal notices
Other	Others	Anti-money laundering / KYC policy

KYC = know-your-customer.
Source: Deloitte.

Figure 7: Typical Process for Document Extraction

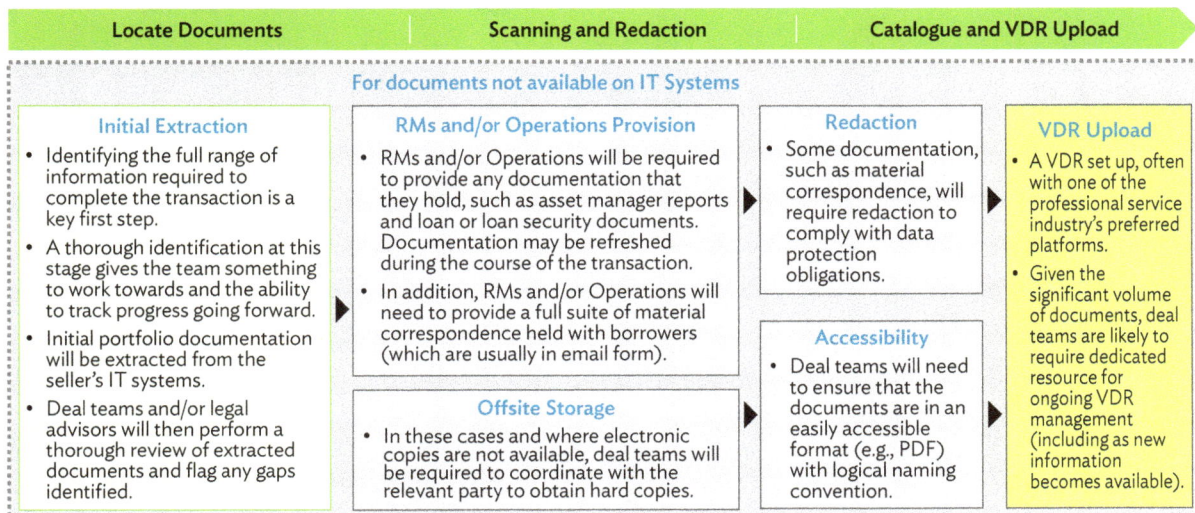

Locate Documents	Scanning and Redaction	Catalogue and VDR Upload

For documents not available on IT Systems

Initial Extraction
- Identifying the full range of information required to complete the transaction is a key first step.
- A thorough identification at this stage gives the team something to work towards and the ability to track progress going forward.
- Initial portfolio documentation will be extracted from the seller's IT systems.
- Deal teams and/or legal advisors will then perform a thorough review of extracted documents and flag any gaps identified.

RMs and/or Operations Provision
- RMs and/or Operations will be required to provide any documentation that they hold, such as asset manager reports and loan or loan security documents. Documentation may be refreshed during the course of the transaction.
- In addition, RMs and/or Operations will need to provide a full suite of material correspondence held with borrowers (which are usually in email form).

Offsite Storage
- In these cases and where electronic copies are not available, deal teams will be required to coordinate with the relevant party to obtain hard copies.

Redaction
- Some documentation, such as material correspondence, will require redaction to comply with data protection obligations.

Accessibility
- Deal teams will need to ensure that the documents are in an easily accessible format (e.g., PDF) with logical naming convention.

VDR Upload
- A VDR set up, often with one of the professional service industry's preferred platforms.
- Given the significant volume of documents, deal teams are likely to require dedicated resource for ongoing VDR management (including as new information becomes available).

IT = information technology, RM = relationship manager, VDR = virtual data room.
Source: Deloitte.

Historically, information required for investor due diligence would have been hosted in physical deal rooms. Since the global financial crisis, records have become increasingly available in digital form; this varies in practice possibly to a significant extent. Unsecured portfolios tend to be less document heavy, and may more easily lend themselves to digitization needed for online trading.

C.   Prerequisites for a Functioning Secondary Market for Nonperforming Loans

When considering what are the prerequisites for functioning secondary markets, it may be insightful first to highlight the features that typify underdeveloped secondary markets, as reflected in several countries across the region (Figure 8).

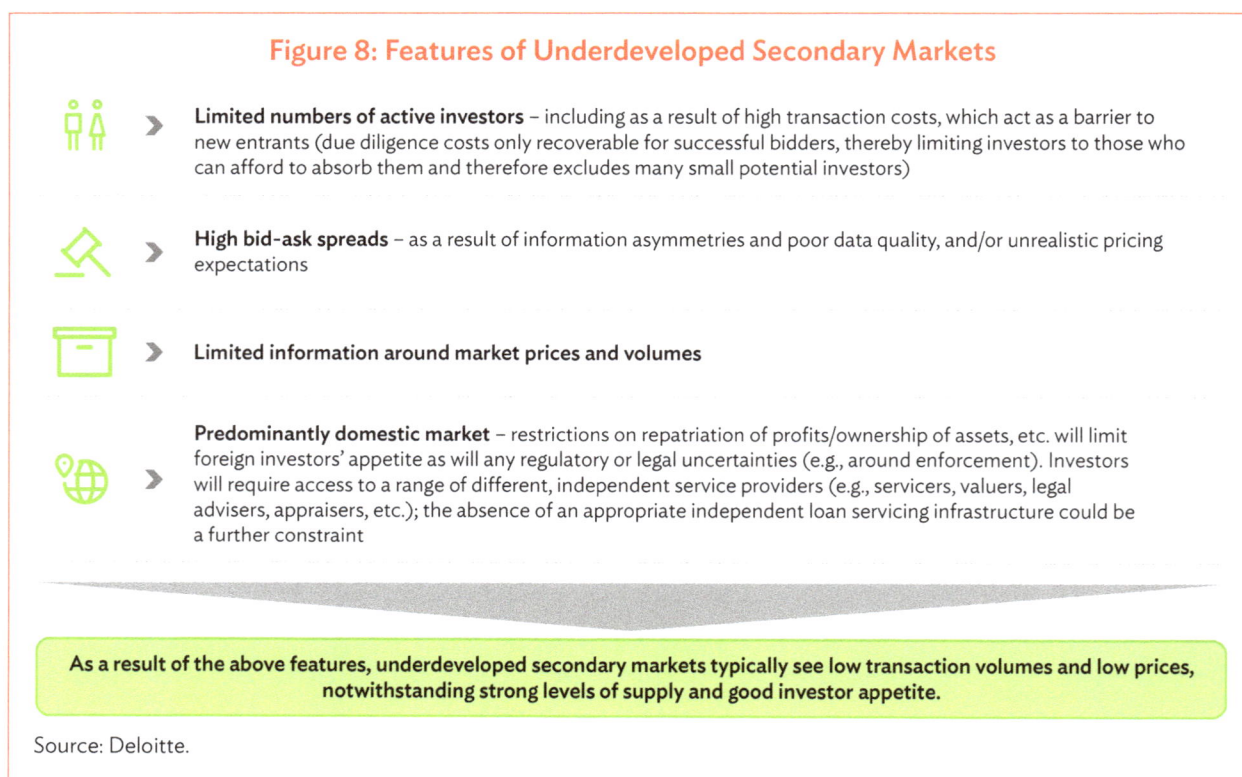

Figure 8: Features of Underdeveloped Secondary Markets

Limited numbers of active investors – including as a result of high transaction costs, which act as a barrier to new entrants (due diligence costs only recoverable for successful bidders, thereby limiting investors to those who can afford to absorb them and therefore excludes many small potential investors)

High bid-ask spreads – as a result of information asymmetries and poor data quality, and/or unrealistic pricing expectations

Limited information around market prices and volumes

Predominantly domestic market – restrictions on repatriation of profits/ownership of assets, etc. will limit foreign investors' appetite as will any regulatory or legal uncertainties (e.g., around enforcement). Investors will require access to a range of different, independent service providers (e.g., servicers, valuers, legal advisers, appraisers, etc.); the absence of an appropriate independent loan servicing infrastructure could be a further constraint

As a result of the above features, underdeveloped secondary markets typically see low transaction volumes and low prices, notwithstanding strong levels of supply and good investor appetite.

Source: Deloitte.

Considerations for Investors

Broadening the number of market participants will bring benefits, including additional liquidity. Investors will require several key questions answered before entering a market. Alternatively, they are likely to remain limited to a small number of (principally domestic) participants only, which will inhibit sellers' ability to divest NPLs and negatively affect pricing. These may be summarized as follows:

Size of opportunity. Some markets may be considered too small or the duration of the opportunity too short to invest time in developing. Given the time required to develop a presence in the market, a visible pipeline of future deals will be important.

Maturity of markets. Less mature markets typically carry higher rates of return to compensate for perceived higher risk and, therefore, dependent on risk appetite may appeal to certain investors compared to lower risk, lower return, more established markets.

Information asymmetry. On the demand side, this represents a potential significant barrier to entry. Banks have an information advantage over investors in the quality of NPLs, leading to an outcome where only low-quality assets are traded. Investors with limited information would use a much higher discount rate in evaluating the value of NPLs, creating wide *bid-ask* spreads. Moreover, the absence of established capacity to value impaired assets and conduct the necessary due diligence and licensing requirements may act as a further deterrent to investors.

Supply side impediments. Too wide a gap between what price buyers are prepared to pay and what sellers are ready to accept will inhibit transaction activity. Thus, the reluctance of banks to accept losses, coupled with inappropriate provisioning approaches, will act as an impediment to effective NPL resolution. Sellers need to be realistic.

Structural issues. Investors buy on the premise that they will be able to more effectively recover against borrowers who are not performing than the originating bank. This could be for a number of reasons, including the willingness and/or ability to take a more aggressive approach to debt collection, economies of scale, or regulatory issues (e.g., in relation to capital requirements). Structural issues, such as the legal or regulatory framework, can act as a significant barrier to entry.

Complex, overburdened legal systems and lengthy judicial processes act to discourage investors from investing in distressed assets, because the enforcement of the collateral and the outcome of insolvency proceedings could be significantly delayed, costly, and/or unpredictable. Moreover, if debtors are aware that the collateral will not be easily and quickly enforced, they may feel less incentivized to pay their loans in a timely manner.

Equally, weak debt enforcement increases costs of collection and prevents banks or investors from seizing the collateral in a timely manner, ultimately leading to a wider bid-ask spread.

Legal requirements (rules for the transfer of credit contracts or restrictions on purchasers of NPLs) may also prevent or significantly restrict the development of a secondary market for NPLs, including in terms of activities that foreign investors may engage in. In some countries, a loan may only be transferred with the explicit prior consent of the debtor.

Rights to collateral may be affected in a similar way. Likewise, data privacy laws may restrict the provision of loan (and the borrower) information.

Requisites for a Functioning Nonperforming Loan Market

Functioning NPL markets therefore depend upon:

- an appropriate legal framework for debt collection and collateral enforcement, which provides balanced protections for borrowers and lenders, including sufficient court capacity to resolve disputes;

- developed loan-servicing and debt-collection infrastructure, providing sufficient depth and breadth of expertise for servicing and restructuring activities required to rehabilitate debtors and collect against amounts due;
- good quality, available, financial and nonfinancial data;
- established capacity for valuation and due diligence when transacting; and
- a liquid market for underlying collateral assets and appropriate, as well as available, finance.

The presence or otherwise of these elements across the region is further considered in Chapter III, which also includes an evaluation of different jurisdictions' readiness for the development of an online NPL trading platform.

III. Criteria for Assessment of Identified Economies' Capacity for Nonperforming Loan Trading

Despite some momentum in recent years, with notable exceptions, NPL secondary markets remain largely underdeveloped in the Asian region. Liquidity and depth are still rather modest, bid-ask spreads rather high and regulatory impediments hamper NPL trading (Figure 9).

Figure 9: Bid-Ask Spreads in Asia—Difference between Net Book Value and Estimated Bid Price

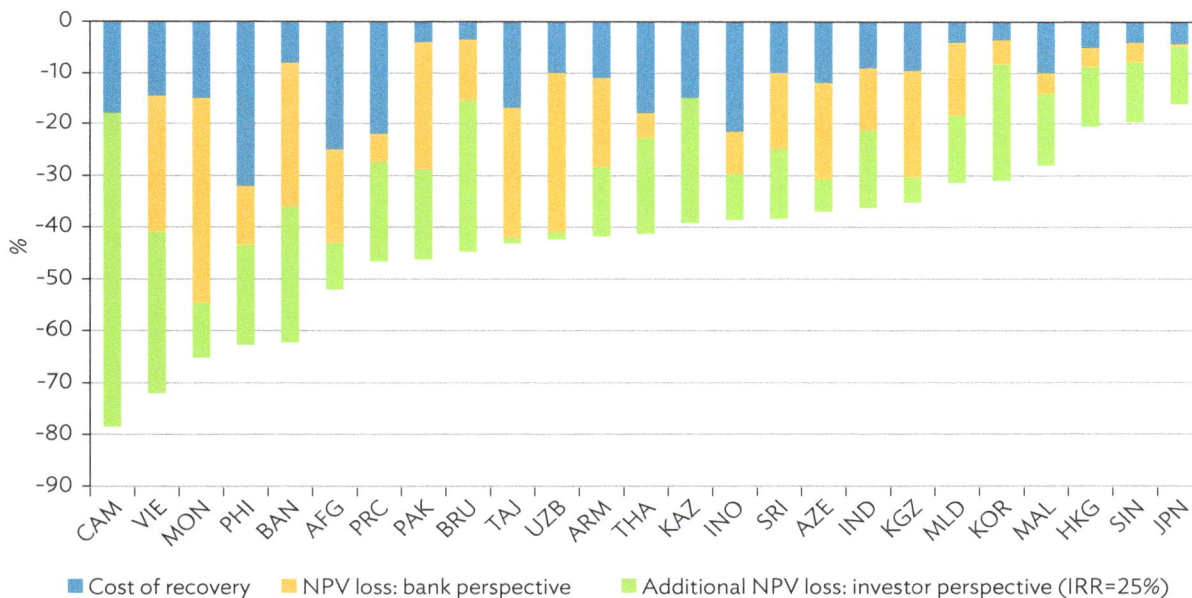

Legend: Cost of recovery; NPV loss: bank perspective; Additional NPV loss: investor perspective (IRR=25%)

AFG = Afghanistan; ARM = Armenia; AZE = Azerbaijan; BAN = Bangladesh; BRU = Brunei Darussalam; CAM = Cambodia; HKG = Hong Kong, China; IND = India; INO = Indonesia; IRR = internal rate of return; JPN = Japan; KAZ = Kazakhstan; KOR = Republic of Korea; KGZ = Kyrgyz Republic; MAL = Malaysia; MLD = Maldives; MON = Mongolia; NPV = net present value; PAK = Pakistan; PHI = Philippines; PRC = People's Republic of China; SIN = Singapore; SRI = Sri Lanka; TAJ = Tajikistan; THA = Thailand; UZB = Uzbekistan; VIE = Viet Nam.

Notes:
1. For Cambodia and Kazakhstan, only the total NPV loss is reported, without being separated into bank perspective and investor perspective. The bank lending rate data are not available in these countries.
2. The Asian Development Bank (ADB) placed on hold its assistance in Afghanistan, effective 15 August 2021 (ADB. 2021. ADB Statement on Afghanistan. News release. 10 November).

Source: Lee, J., C. Y. Park, D. Park, and P. Rosenkranz. 2021. Strategies for Developing Asia's Nonperforming Loan Markets and Resolution Mechanisms. In J. Fell, M. Grodzicki, J. Lee, R. Martin, C. Y. Park, and P. Rosenkranz, eds. *Nonperforming Loans in Asia and Europe—Causes, Impacts, and Resolution Strategies*. Manila: ADB.

This is compounded by market shortcomings, such as information asymmetries. Potential buyers may not have access to reliable, granular, readily available standardized information on asset quality and loan tapes in banks. Consequently, potential buyers may bid a purchase price that does not reflect the value of portfolios for sale, hindering potential transactions. Thus, banks need to be incentivized to improve the data quality and to disclose more information on NPLs.

Selection Criteria and Assessment

Building on analysis set out in Chapter II, including prerequisites for a functioning secondary market for NPL and investor requirements in terms of domestic and cross-border trading, the following factors appear relevant in determining which markets may benefit most from and are potentially ready for the introduction of online NPL trading platforms:

Absolute and relative levels of nonperforming loans. From an investor perspective, the larger the market the more interest it may generate. The PRC has by far the largest stock of NPLs in the region. That said, markets with high NPL ratios should (relatively speaking) benefit most from a deepening of secondary markets, notwithstanding lower levels in absolute terms—e.g., Mongolia (10.0%), Pakistan (8.3%), Bangladesh (8.2%) in 2021, as shown in Table 2.

Existing track record of nonperforming loan trading. Given the costs of development and set up, investors and platform operators will be more attracted to already existing markets. The PRC, Thailand, the Republic of Korea, Indonesia, the Philippines, Viet Nam, and Malaysia have (to a greater or lesser extent) active NPL markets; whereas, other countries in the region have limited or no experience. The Kazakhstan market, for instance, is considered by local market participants surveyed for this study (footnote 1) to be only somewhat active—trades happen mainly between commercial banks and the Fund for Problem Loans—with few major transactions taking place in recent years. As a result, the Government of Kazakhstan has initiated the creation of a working group to study the development of a national NPL market.

Legal frameworks conducive to nonperforming loan resolution and collateral enforcement. Foreclosure and debt enforcement practices vary considerably across Asian countries in terms of their effectiveness and duration. For instance, according to World Bank's Doing Business Resolving Insolvency (2015 and 2019), in Viet Nam, the average period for foreclosure and enforcement is said to be around 5 years; whereas, in other countries, it may be quicker.

Reflecting on the above considerations, an illustrative points-based system was used to select the markets, which may benefit most from, and be more ready for development of, an online trading platform, as set out in Tables 9 and 10.[4]

Applying the scoring framework in Table 9, the PRC, Thailand, the Republic of Korea, Indonesia, and Kazakhstan, all of which achieved a score of at least 3 out of a maximum of 8 points, were identified as most likely to benefit from or be most ready (to varying degrees) for the development of an online NPL trading platform as an additional tool for NPL resolution.[5]

---

[4]   Other factors also need to be considered including, for instance, independent servicing capacity; the aforementioned considerations form a starting point. Chapter IV provides a further discussion on this matter.

[5]   Australia, India, Japan, and Singapore were considered outside the remit of the study.

Table 9: Illustrative Scoring Basis

Factors for Scoring	Range of Scores
NPL stock	• Greater than $200 billion = 3 points • $75.00 billion–$199.99 billion = 2 points • $15.00 billion–$74.99 billion = 1 point
NPL ratio	• More than 7% = 2 points • 2.00%–6.99% = 1 point
Whether an active market already exists	• Some experience of NPL trading = 1 point
Effectiveness of the legal framework	• The World Bank's Doing Business Resolving Insolvency rankings (2019) were considered. • Scores of above 60 = 1 point • Scores 40.00–59.99 = 0.5 point
Already existing NPL or collateral trading platforms	• 1 point for yes • Otherwise, zero points
Advanced economies	• Out of scope

NPL = nonperforming loan.

Source: Authors' compilation.

Table 10: Illustrative Rankings of Readiness for an Online Nonperforming Loan Transaction Platform

Country	DMC	Active Public AMC	World Bank Classification	Region	NPL Stock	NPL Stock Score	NPL Ratio	NPL Ratio Score	Historical NPL Trade	Online Platform Already	"Strength of Legal Framework" World Bank Score	Legal Framework Score	Total
Australia	Advanced Economy	N	High Income	Pacific	23.1	1.0	1.0%	–	1.0	–	78.9	1.0	3.0
Azerbaijan	DMC	N	Upper Middle	Central and West Asia	0.5	–	4.6%	1.0	–	–	63.5	1.0	2.0
Bangladesh	DMC	N	Lower Middle	South Asia	11.8	–	8.2%	2.0	–	–	28.1	–	2.0
Cambodia	DMC	N	Lower Middle	Southeast Asia	0.9	–	2.1%	1.0	–	–	48.5	0.5	1.5
People's Republic of China	DMC	Y	Upper Middle	East Asia	447.9	3.0	1.7%	–	1.0	1.0	62.1	1.0	6.0
India	DMC	N	Lower Middle	South Asia	109.6	2.0	6.9%	1.0	1.0	–	62.0	1.0	5.0
Indonesia	DMC	Y	Upper Middle	Southeast Asia	12.7	–	3.0%	1.0	1.0	–	68.1	1.0	3.0
Japan	Advanced Economy	N	High Income	East Asia	114.6	2.0	1.5%	–	1.0	–	90.2	1.0	4.0
Kazakhstan	DMC	Y	Upper Middle	Central and West Asia	1.7	–	4.8%	1.0	–	1.0	66.7	1.0	3.0
Republic of Korea	Graduated DMC	Y	High Income	East Asia	9.8	–	0.5%	–	1.0	1.0	82.9	1.0	3.0
Malaysia	DMC	Y	Upper Middle	Southeast Asia	6.6	–	1.5%	–	1.0	–	67.0	1.0	2.0
Mongolia	DMC	N	Lower Middle	East Asia	0.7	–	10.0%	2.0	–	–	30.1	–	2.0
Nepal	DMC	N	Lower Middle	South Asia	0.5	–	1.4%	–	–	–	47.2	0.5	0.5
New Zealand	Advanced Economy	N	High Income	Pacific	0.9	–	0.3%	–	–	–	69.5	1.0	1.0
Pakistan	DMC	N	Lower Middle	Central and West Asia	5.1	–	8.3%	2.0	–	–	59.0	0.5	2.5
Philippines	DMC	N	Lower Middle	Southeast Asia	9.5	–	4.4%	1.0	1.0	–	55.1	0.5	2.5
Singapore	Graduated DMC	N	High Income	Southeast Asia	22.3	1.0	2.3%	1.0	–	–	74.3	1.0	3.0
Sri Lanka	DMC	N	Lower Middle	South Asia	2.5	–	5.0%	1.0	–	–	45.0	0.5	1.5

continued on next page

Table 10 *continued*

Country	DMC	Active Public AMC	World Bank Classification	Region	NPL Stock	NPL Stock Score	NPL Ratio	NPL Ratio Score	Historical NPL Trade	Online Platform Already	"Strength of Legal Framework" World Bank Score	Legal Framework Score	Total
Thailand	DMC	Y	Upper Middle	Southeast Asia	16.2	1.0	3.1%	1.0	1.0	–	76.8	1.0	4.0
Uzbekistan	DMC	N	Lower Middle	Central and West Asia	1.7	–	5.7%	1.0	–	–	43.5	0.5	1.5
Viet Nam	DMC	Y	Lower Middle	Southeast Asia	6.3	–	1.7%	–	1.0	–	38.0	–	1.0

– = zero score, AMC = asset management company, DMC = developing member country, N = No, NPL = nonperforming loan, Y = Yes.

Note: Using the scoring system above, countries in green were selected for further study. Both Kazakhstan and Viet Nam governments have announced their intentions to investigate the steps necessary to develop NPL markets, including the prospect of cross-border trading and the development of an online NPL trading platform.

Sources: Asian Development Bank, World Bank, International Monetary Fund, central banks, and prudential authorities.

IV. Feasibility for Nonperforming Loan Trading

Considering the assessed economies in the region within the scope of this study,[6] the PRC, Thailand, the Republic of Korea, and Indonesia already have experience of domestic NPL trading. This includes some limited, cross-border trading; although, NPL markets in each are at differing stages of maturity, which could benefit from the introduction of an online NPL trading platform. Equally, while the NPL market in Kazakhstan is undeveloped, NPL levels are relatively high, and the Government of Kazakhstan has set up a working group to evaluate the further development of the NPL market both domestically and for cross-border trading. Viet Nam has announced a similar initiative. As such, the rest of this chapter focuses on these countries and considers the requirements for NPL trading, including cross-border trading and the involvement of foreign investors in domestic NPL markets.

Of the other countries previously considered, while Malaysia has an established legal framework, NPL stocks are relatively low and thus the country may (perhaps) be of lesser interest to foreign investors compared to other jurisdictions.

However, by initially focusing on certain countries only, that should not preclude other economies participating in the proposed initiative or joining at a later stage when conditions are met.

A. Existing and Possible Legal Requisites and Conditions for Nonperforming Loan Trading

In general, the legal requisites and conditions for well-functioning NPL markets vary widely across countries in the region, with a general lack of guidance and established legal framework around NPL resolution methods and loan sales. Governments are, however, taking steps to address this, as in Kazakhstan where a government-led working group has been set up to consider the steps necessary for the development of the NPL market in the country.

A supportive framework for NPL sales and a creditor-friendly legal regime for restructuring, collection, enforcement, and insolvency are fundamental for a functioning NPL market.

Lengthy and complex enforcement processes create uncertainty, increase collection costs, and ultimately lead to a wider bid-ask spread for NPL sales. The nature of the legal processes for execution proceedings, collateral enforcement action, laws on insolvency, and the bankruptcy system in each country will be important stimulus factors for building a cross-border NPL trading platform.

---

[6] For the purposes of this study, advanced economies in the region (where governments are expected to take their own initiatives) were excluded.

Countries with more developed and effective processes, as well as timely, easier, and faster procedures will be more attractive to investors.

Nevertheless, the development of an NPL Online Trading Platform in Asian countries to the level that meets international standards will take time, while investors conduct research on related laws and regulations of each country before making an investment in a given region.

Table 11 provides a high-level assessment of the relative development of legal frameworks for debt collection, collateral enforcement, and NPL trading.

Table 11: Country Summary for Existing and Possible Legal Requisites and Conditions for Nonperforming Loan Trading

Jurisdiction	Legal Framework Assessment	Comments
People's Republic of China	Developing	The enforcement process can still take up between 18 to 42 months, depending on the status of the security (whether it is seized by the creditor) and the location of the assets.
Republic of Korea and Thailand	Established	The Republic of Korea and Thailand are considered to have relatively established legal frameworks for nonperforming loan (NPL) resolutions, with legal frameworks and relevant infrastructures having been established and refined since the Asian financial crisis.
Indonesia	Developing	While the market has seen several NPL transactions in recent years, further development of the NPL market is hindered by ongoing uncertainty around legal enforcement procedures and portfolio transaction regulations, with a lack of guidance from regulators on NPL management and disposition approaches. Restrictions imposed on state banks prohibit selling NPLs below par value.
Viet Nam	Immature	Enforcement proceedings in Viet Nam can be lengthy, from several months to several years. Viet Nam Asset Management Company is leading a review of the legal framework for resolution of NPLs, and the government is considering other steps necessary for NPL market development.
Kazakhstan	Immature	The Government of Kazakhstan has commenced a project to develop NPL markets in the country, including the development of an online platform for cross-border trading, and is receiving technical assistance from the European Bank for Reconstruction and Development.

Source: Authors' compilation, based on the World Bank's Doing Business Resolving Insolvency Survey and views of market participants.

In terms of legal requisites, the platform may be subject to fintech-related law (e.g., the Electronic Financial Transaction Act in the Republic of Korea) and consumer data protection law, in addition to any existing regulations for NPL trading, which should be considered in the design phase. Given the varying levels of development of legal frameworks for NPL trading differ between countries in the region, a harmonized process along with appropriate best practice guidance may aide the smooth functioning of cross-border transaction platforms.

B. Overview of Current Policies and Mechanisms on Sale of Nonperforming Loans to Foreign Investors and Cross-Border Trading

Foreign involvement in NPL markets can bring benefits through additional liquidity injection into the financial system and management expertise in resolving bad debts. However, in many jurisdictions, legislative frameworks are generally protectionist, including in ownership and licensing.

In some economies in Asia, such as Cambodia; the PRC; Hong Kong, China; Malaysia; Singapore; and Viet Nam, 100% foreign ownership is allowed. Nevertheless, in certain sectors, a local shareholder or business partner is required. In many other economies, a certain degree of local ownership is required, either for all industries or for certain sectors.

As a consequence, NPL markets in Asia tend to be dominated by domestic players, with a small number of international investors operating only in more mature markets, such as the PRC and the Republic of Korea, and even then, with a very small share of the market. While the underlying reasons for this vary, immature legal frameworks (including around NPL transfers and enforcement processes), restrictions on foreign ownership (including of collateral), and inefficient capital markets act as deterrent to new foreign entrants who generally take a cautious approach (Table 12).

Table 12: Nonperforming Loan Market Activity

Jurisdiction	NPL Market Status	Comments
Republic of Korea	Mature —significant historical foreign involvement	International investors have been less active in recent years, reflecting a relatively stable NPL market, lower NPL levels (compared to during the Asian financial crisis), which banks are generally able to resolve for themselves, and low returns. An increase in NPLs triggered by COVID-19 is likely to revive foreign interest in the Republic of Korea NPL market, which has no restrictions toward NPL buyers from overseas.
People's Republic of China	Developed —limited international involvement	NPL investors from outside of the People's Republic of China remain cautious in NPL market activity and pricing, reflecting an unfamiliar legal environment. Commercial banks can only sell NPLs to AMCs, which must be licensed. There are no restrictions on NPL buyers from AMCs; currency and capital control regulations, and foreign ownership restrictions act as a deterrent for overseas investors. In recent times, several foreign companies have or are seeking to establish joint ventures or partnership arrangements to operate as private AMCs. This is still developing, but offers the prospect of greater involvement in the future.
Indonesia	Developing —limited international involvement	Foreign investors have been actively exploring opportunities in the local NPL markets, and there have been several cross-border deals around distressed asset investments in Indonesia. However, there remain significant limitations, which act to deter active investing, including foreign ownership restrictions and uncertainties in the legal and regulatory frameworks.

continued on next page

Table 12 *continued*

Jurisdiction	NPL Market Status	Comments
Viet Nam and Kazakhstan	Immature —no international involvement	Positive signs of state authorities seeking to attract foreign capital to the local NPL market. In Viet Nam, an electronic NPL trading platform is being developed, aimed at both domestic and overseas buyers. However, the country is yet to improve the legal framework around NPL transfers, and other policy developments are potentially contradictory (see Chapter IV, section D on pp. 35–36 on Servicing Infrastructure). In Kazakhstan, a government-led working group, supported by international development organizations, has been looking to develop a secondary NPL market by introducing appropriate regulations and joining a cross-border NPL trading platform to attract foreign investors.

AMC = asset management company, COVID-19 = coronavirus disease, NPL = nonperforming loan.
Source: Market participants.

Work is still required to develop legal frameworks and infrastructure in a number of countries to the stage whereby respective NPL markets will be of significant interest to international investors. Moreover, in many jurisdictions, there is no level playing field as between international and domestic investors, which would need to be remedied to attract foreign capital.

Similarly, although not studied in detail in this report, currency and capital control regulations may operate as an impediment. This should be considered further.

C. Nonperforming Loan Recognition and Valuation Standards

Trading of NPLs is dependent on the harmonization of NPL recognition and valuation standards, particularly for cross-border trading. While some progress has been made toward this, a number of major regional economies and holders of NPLs continue to use incurred loss standards, with no timetable decided upon for introduction of recognized international standards. This may act as a deterrent to investors looking to enter the market and creates practical difficulties from a cross-border transaction perspective.

Moreover, in several jurisdictions, legal restrictions to protect taxpayers and guard against embezzlement risk and cultural differences may result in pricing gaps, with sellers unwilling or unable to take a loss on disposals. Insufficient provisioning or different provisioning approaches can have the same effect, limiting transaction activity notwithstanding strong supply and demand factors.

D. Servicing Infrastructure

Appropriate depth and breadth of loan-servicing infrastructure are important for both domestic and international NPL investors. International investors, in particular, may tend to rely significantly on third-party loan servicers and debt collection agencies, while major local AMCs primarily rely on their own resources. Moreover, management of secured loans (corporates, SMEs, retails, housing) and unsecured loans have different human capital and technology development requirements. Managing secured loans needs more financial and negotiation skills, while managing unsecured loans needs more soft skills and automated transaction systems.

Loan servicing and debt collection capabilities vary across countries under review. However, the general trend across financial institutions and AMCs in Asia is that NPLs are usually worked out in-house rather than outsourced to third-party servicers. The decision to use third-party companies also depends on the type of NPL, secured or unsecured, with secured loans being more likely serviced internally with the expectation of greater returns from the underlying collateral sale.

In the PRC, due to issues around change of legal title, certain sellers (e.g., state-owned AMCs) may keep servicing NPLs as they may be better placed to work them out more efficiently than private investors (e.g., faster legal proceedings, access to technology). The loan-servicing market in the PRC appears to be developing faster than in neighboring countries, including with international involvement.

Similarly, Collectius, a Singapore-based unsecured debt collection company operating across several Asian states, has recently announced its partnership with International Finance Corporation to develop a platform to manage and resolve unsecured debt in the Association of Southeast Asian Nations region.

By contrast, since January 2021, debt collection businesses can no longer operate in Viet Nam due to concerns including inappropriate collection practices.[7] For similar reasons, debt collectors in Kazakhstan are not considered particularly efficient, with a recovery ratio ranging between 25% and 30%. Likewise, in Indonesia, debt collection activity is largely unregulated, with plenty of small debt collection agencies.

A lack of or inefficient debt collection resource is likely to impede the development of secondary NPL markets in Asia as debt servicing would be available to major investors only, especially regarding funding and manpower required to efficiently work out NPLs. International development organizations may be able to help motivate, start to encourage initiative, or provide technical assistance to promote local AMCs and improve their capacity and efficiency to be able to provide servicing to international NPL investors.

Regulation of Loan Servicers and Debt Collection Agencies

Regulators need to balance appropriate and sustainable collection practices that protect consumers and borrowers with industry standards that do not restrict lenders' ability to efficiently work out NPLs.

Another important factor to consider for a cross-border debt trading platform is harmonized standards of loan servicing and debt collection across participating nations. By way of example, the European Commission has published a Directive on Credit Servicers and Credit Purchasers that aims to regulate and harmonize the credit servicing industry across all European Union member states to further encourage the development of the secondary NPL market.

In an Asian context, similar steps might need to be taken to open up and harmonize the credit servicing industry and, ultimately, to facilitate cross-border NPL trading.

---

[7]   *HD Law & FDICO Law Firm.* 2020. Viet Nam Will Ban the Debt Collection Service. 24 June.

E.   Legal Framework for Nonperforming Loans Securitization

NPL securitizations can be useful in resolving high NPLs; credit enhancement is often required for senior tranches and they can be structurally complex to set up, requiring significant due diligence.

As anticipated, the use of securitization structures for NPL resolution closely correlates with NPL level and capital market development. The PRC and the Republic of Korea have each seen NPL securitization transactions in the past, while other countries such as Indonesia, Kazakhstan, and Thailand have not yet observed significant (or any) NPL securitization activity. Moreover, in Viet Nam, there is currently no applicable framework allowing for the use of NPLs in securitization structures.

However, this should not present a fundamental roadblock either to the development of a market for NPLs or for the development of an online trading platform. Functioning NPL markets existed for many years in other countries before NPLs were accepted as collateral for securitizations—and even now, only relatively few countries (e.g., Greece and Italy) use them widely. In markets where securitizations have historically played an important role in NPL resolution (e.g., the Republic of Korea), NPL securitizations could, of course, be included as one of the asset classes traded on the online platform.

F.   Legal Foundation of Asset Management Companies to Realize Profits from Intermediating Nonperforming Loans Sales to Foreign Investors

As discussed in Chapter I, public AMCs play an important role in helping banks clean up their balance sheets and, in general, financial stability. Moreover, while public AMCs operate primarily to collect old outstanding bad debts acquired from financial institutions, all AMCs interviewed for this study emphasized they should do so in a socially responsible manner to support borrowers as far as possible (footnote 1). Generally, enforcement is reserved for borrowers who fail to cooperate or as a last resort.

As to whether public AMCs can or should sell NPLs at a profit, NPL sales play an important role in freeing up AMC's capital and generating additional liquidity, thereby allowing them to take more bad loans out of the banking system without increasing the level of taxpayer support required. Transacting through an online platform can make this a more efficient process both in terms of time to complete and from a pricing perspective. Moreover, with appropriate borrower protections in place to guard against unsustainable collection practices, covering all credit purchasers and servicers, this would not conflict with public AMCs' broader aim to treat borrowers fairly.

G. Relationship and Dynamics between Platform Founders or Operators and Platform Participants

Success of the platforms will depend on its ability to gain a critical mass of users and generate economies of scale. In turn, this will depend on users having confidence in the platform, including in terms of its processes. This may be best achieved if the platform is independent of holders of NPLs; although, AMCs may still wish to develop their own platforms for disposals.

Alternative ownership structures are discussed in Chapter V, section G (pp. 44–45).

V. Practical Considerations in Developing a Nonperforming Loan Platform

This chapter considers the practical considerations for establishing an online NPL trading platform, including in terms of functionality and ancillary services provided by or through the platform, scope of the platform (in terms of geographic reach and asset perimeter), data consistency (templates) and quality (validation tools), ownership, and governance.

A.   Functionality and Ancillary Services

As discussed in Chapter I, for this feasibility study, it has been assumed that the activities of an online NPL transaction platform for the Asian region would comprise:

- Marketing portfolios of NPLs and potentially other noncore assets, including **matching buyers and sellers**—Buyers and sellers should be able to connect with each other through the platform. Existing platforms include the option for investors to specify their transaction preferences and for targeted "push" notifications when new portfolios are uploaded onto the system on behalf of sellers.
- **Data warehousing**—The platform would operate as an online, regularly updated data warehouse (or virtual data room), which investors can access for due diligence purposes. The following could be two possible models:
    - either the platform could operate as a one stop shop, to house all financial and nonfinancial data required for due diligence purposes; or
    - the platform could house financial data only, and perhaps at a higher (template-based) level for initial pricing purposes; thereafter, investors wishing to submit a binding offer could approach the seller directly for more detailed financial and nonfinancial data and due diligence.
- In any event, platforms should incorporate **automated quality checks** to ensure completeness and plausibility of the data being hosted (discussed in more detail below).
- **Bidding and online auction**—May be either open and visible to all parties or sealed (other bidders cannot see what is being offered).
- **Intermediating between investors and other third-party service providers**—e.g., valuers, providers of due diligence and other related services including legal advisers, credit servicers, debt collection agents, (potentially) finance providers, etc.

For ancillary services, to keep operating costs down, the platform would act as intermediary rather than as a provider of such services. Subject to the platform reaching a critical mass, third-party service providers may be prepared to pay a listing or introduction fee, which could be passed on to platform users in the form of lower charges generally.

B. Geographic Reach

A key objective of the platform is to reduce transaction costs, which might otherwise exclude smaller market participants. This may be best achieved by maximizing the number of users and generating economies of scale. This implies that, for certain smaller markets at least, a platform capable of dealing with transactions on a regional basis should be the overall aim. In this way, sellers of NPLs in smaller markets, which otherwise might not attract significant investor interest, could potentially bundle their NPLs with other loans to create larger more saleable portfolios.

That said, NPL markets in different jurisdictions are not all at the same stages of development, with some countries potentially requiring significant legal reforms, including to collateral enforcement and asset ownership regimes, to attract investors and create a functioning market. As such, development of a regional platform may best be attempted in a multiphased approach, focusing first on those countries that are ready for it (e.g., the PRC, the Republic of Korea, Thailand, etc.), with other countries joining later, when the necessary conditions are met. This should not prevent other less mature markets nevertheless seeking to develop, which may be assisted by way of knowledge transfer from other more mature markets.

C. Asset Perimeter

For similar reasons, it seems appropriate to aim for as broad a scope of assets traded on the platform as possible. There is no reason (in principle) why noncore assets generally (i.e., not just NPLs) including performing portfolios could not be offered on the platform. Many portfolio sales are, in fact, a mix of performing and nonperforming or reperforming loans (Table 13).

Table 13: Considerations by Asset Type

Key Considerations	

Secured / Unsecured	• Considering the trading of secured loans on the online platform:
	  – Documentation and data availability/requirements are relatively well understood.
	  – There is generally good supply held by the banks to sustain the pipeline.
	  – It is generally easier to price a collateralized NPL than an unsecured one in secondary markets as the value of the collateral sets the minimum value of an NPL.

Retail / Corporate	• Retail portfolios would benefit from the homogeneity of underlying loan products and borrowers. The loan files are usually standardized with limited customized terms for each individual loans. • However, in some countries, banks already work with DCAs to dispose of their unsecured retail loans on a regular basis, and an online trading platform may add little value to the process. • Regulatory requirements need to be considered when trading in consumer books. • Corporate loans (including special lending) could have multiple lender relationships where a single borrower may be indebted to several banks. Lack of coordination between banks may add to the difficulty in the transaction and resolution of such loans. • In addition, documentation requirements are usually more complex for corporate loans and special lending compared to retail loans. Buyers may expect to see evidence on the operation and solvency status of the company and/or the assets/projects.
Narrow / Broad	• NPL platforms look to benefit from realizing economies of scale and scope, and as such may best be achieved by considering a broad range of asset classes to the extent practical. The scope may also be extended to include performing loans to attract different types of investors. It may be appropriate to start with a narrower focus and then gradually open up as the platform develops.
Regional / National	• Investors can enjoy the benefits of diversification on a cross-border regional trading platform, which pool assets from several jurisdictions. However, specific national data needs, regulations, and different legal enforcement frameworks across countries would need to be taken into account.

DCA = debt collection agency, NPL = nonperforming loan.

Source: Authors' compilation.

For ease of use, assets should be grouped into homogenous groups, such as

- commercial real estate assets,
- residential real estate assets,
- SMEs or other corporate loans,
- unsecured retail loans,
- asset-backed finance,
- car loans, and
- other/specialized NPLs.

Notably, some jurisdictions restrict the types of asset that may be traded. For instance, in Thailand, the AMC Act allows only NPL to be transferred and/or sold.

As noted, transaction platforms typically offer optionality around the bidding process for better execution, which could include single bid, bucket, cherry picking, and whole-tranche bids.

The platform will need to be fully compliant with all relevant personal data and banking secrecy laws for the countries in which it operates. While ultimately all types of loan could be accepted onto the platform, certain sectors or types may more readily be transacted on the platform and could form an initial focus. For instance, corporate loans are easier to handle than consumer or mortgage loans given the application of personal data and consumer protection rules to consumer or mortgage loans. In the same way, consumer or mortgage loans are more standardized and, hence, potentially better suited to being traded centrally on an NPL platform than, for example, SME loans.

D.   Data Consistency (Templates)

Investors require good quality data for pricing and decision making. A key objective of the platform is to reduce information asymmetries and lower transaction costs, thereby mitigating potential barriers to entry and opening up the NPL market in the region to a broader investor base, including smaller investors who might otherwise find themselves priced out of the market by high due diligence costs.

Standardized data templates can help with this, enhancing granularity, quality, and comparability of NPL data as well as providing increased transparency, thereby supporting the development of a functioning NPL secondary market. Cost savings can be achieved through a more efficient and smoother due diligence process—buyers get the information they need, and sellers know up front what information is expected and can therefore incorporate it into their loan systems architecture. Major challenges include creating data-mapping templates and data validation, which is considered in Chapter V, section E (pp. 43–44).

At the same time, standardized templates create a level playing field between different platform operators, fostering fairer competition and setting a minimum standard for information provision.

The revised NPL template proposals of the European Banking Authority (EBA), which have recently been consulted on, could be used as a starting point. It should, however, be recognized that information requirements may differ by jurisdiction and so some tailoring to different markets may be needed (Box 2). As suggested in the EBA consultation paper, the templates could include certain minimum levels of information (for all loans), with additional fields required for completion if certain size criteria are triggered (larger loans). Country-specific requirements could be dealt with in the same way.

Box 2: European Banking Authority Data Templates

The European Banking Authority (EBA) initiated the development of a suite of standardized nonperforming loan (NPL) data templates in 2017 to help facilitate financial due diligence and the valuation of NPL transactions. The aim was to reduce information asymmetries and barriers to entry in the European Union NPL markets, and provide a benchmark for a common data standard for transactions, enabling NPLs to be compared even across jurisdictions. These templates will help address inefficiencies associated with information asymmetries and fragmented approaches across the single market, promote process efficiencies, and reduce transaction costs.

The EBA's initiative on the NPL data templates, including their revision in 2021, is part of a wider action plan to tackle NPLs in Europe. It also provides additional tools for banks in the management and reduction of NPLs on their balance sheets.

In its guidelines on management of nonperforming and forborne exposures, the EBA requires banks to introduce and operationalize NPL reduction strategies. While there are several tools available to banks to manage and reduce NPLs, secondary market transactions are one of these tools. The data templates, therefore, aim to support banks' strategies to manage and reduce their NPLs, particularly in the aftermath of the coronavirus disease (COVID-19) pandemic.

In its December 2020 communication announcing its NPL Action Plan, the European Commission noted that the NPL data templates are not widely used yet by market participants due to their voluntary nature and complexity.

The revised proposals aim to make the existing NPL data templates more user-friendly, less complex, and more proportionate so as to strike the right balance between the cost of information provided and the ability of data users to effectively price the potential transaction.

The NPL data templates are expected to play an important role in addressing the increasing levels of NPLs, particularly in the aftermath of the COVID-19 pandemic and the impact it has on the European Union banking sector.

The discussion paper proposes several changes to the existing templates (such as restructuring of the data categories, designing asset classes, reduction of data fields, and categorization of these data fields as critical and noncritical), and presents proportionality considerations. The revised templates, as presented in the EBA discussion paper, include 230 data fields, reducing the number from 462 in the existing version of the templates; they also reduce the number of critical cells from 155 to a range of 30–70 (depending on the asset class). Data fields cover the same seven asset classes of the existing version of the templates. In addition to these changes, the 17 data categories in the existing version of the templates have been reduced and restructured into five templates to simplify their use for market participants.

———————————

Source: European Banking Authority. 2021. *Discussion Paper on the Review of the NPL Transaction Data Template*. Paris. 4 May.

Should the template be voluntary or made mandatory? Portfolio information (financial data) would be based on standardized templates, drawn from underlying loan tapes, which the seller would prepare.

Requiring market participants to use a standard information template would foster harmonization and generate process efficiencies, thereby reducing overall transaction costs. As discussed in Box 2, besides providing a level of generic information common to all portfolios (distinguished by asset class), additional country-specific fields may be required to cater to local legal requirements. The templates would not necessarily be tied to regulatory reporting. When designing the templates, there would be benefits in a working alongside regulators to reduce the level of new information required.

Recognizing that there will be a cost to completing the templates, it is important that the requirements are kept proportionate to what is actually required for pricing and due diligence (as opposed to what is "nice to have") and to what banks can actually produce.

Given the early stage of development of NPL markets in certain Asian countries, harmonizing data requirements through a standardized NPL template may be easier to achieve than in other more mature markets, with a number of platforms already in operation and where existing practices and/or templates may need to be remodelled.

Should templates be used for new NPLs only or also for existing stocks? As noted above, the templates would form the basis for information stored on the transaction platform and, as such, their use would be a requirement for use of the platform.

Templates could also form the basis for a centralized NPL (post-trade) data depository for analyzing and monitoring overall NPL lifecycle evolution. This could be useful in developing NPL markets more generally (i.e., understanding trends and strategies better), as has been proposed by the European Commission in its December 2020 NPL Action Plan.

There may be benefits for using the templates more broadly (i.e., regardless as to whether the NPLs are to be sold on the platform). Given the cost of preparation, this might require some fiscal incentives that would be balanced by benefit of additional information for policymaking.

Who should take the lead in developing the templates and harmonizing data requirements? Asia does not have the same framework of supranational organizations as in other regions. Coordinating design standards across the different jurisdictions is a central role and one which is perhaps best done either by an international development organization or a multinational industry body.

E.   Data Quality—Financial Data

Ensuring that data populated into the template and available on the platform are of good quality is fundamental to building trust and to keeping due diligence costs low, which will be important in building critical mass. Prior to uploading on the platform, data should be subject to a minimum level of data verification and validation to ensure its accuracy and fitness for purpose. Dependent on the final design of the template, the following could be considered:

Field-Specific Checks

Automated checks are performed across all fields in the template by way of basic validation that the data received are correct and accurate. For example,

- Check that all fields requested in the template are present,
- Check for duplications of unique fields,
- Check the number of missing (blank) values within a given field,
- Check the number of values in incorrect format, and
- Check that values fall within valid ranges.

Cross-Field Checks

For mutually dependent fields within the template (i.e., if a field has a specific value, then the related field must also take a specific value), such as if a loan's number of days past due is greater than 90, it must be flagged as nonperforming exposures according to EBA definition. For example,

- If a collateral item is flagged as property, then the collateral location must be reported; and
- Loan-to-value versus collateral value and loan balance.

Cross-Time Checks

Cross-time checks are performed to ensure the consistency of a dataset across multiple snapshots in time (T0 and T-1). For example,

- If the exposure of the facility in the previous year is positive and the maturity date is before the T0 snapshot, then the exposure is not in the T0 snapshot of the loan tape or the maturity date has been updated as at T0.
- If the facility is > 90 days past due in the T-1 snapshot, then it is flagged as being nonperforming exposures in the last 12 months in the T0 snapshot.

Distribution Checks

This refers to a sense-check on distributions within the data. For example,

- Date fields—skews toward particular time periods should be verified; and
- Remaining maturity—if there is an excess of a particular value, this should be verified.

Input from an experienced platform operator would be beneficial, since such checks should already be incorporated. It should not be necessary to reinvent the wheel.

F.   Availability of Nonfinancial Data for Due Diligence

As discussed in Chapter I, investors rely on both financial and nonfinancial data for due diligence. In many cases, nonfinancial data will be indirectly related to pricing analysis. These kinds of data and documents may have to be manually extracted, cleansed, and catalogued, making for a potentially very labor-intensive process, particularly for large loan portfolios with a significant number of underlying borrowers. Thereafter, for a fully online NPL platform this would need to be digitized and uploaded.

Alternatively, the platform could operate to include just the basic financial data, as well as a more limited suite of nonfinancial information (standard terms and conditions, security documents, etc.) as required for initial due diligence and buyer evaluation (nonbinding offers), with more detailed financial and nonfinancial data made available by the seller to preferred bidders (binding offers). This may be the preferred model, reflecting the cost and timing implications.

G.   Ownership

Several NPL platform ownership alternatives exist dependent on whether the platform is set up as a single regional platform or by individual nations on a domestic basis only.

Nascent NPL markets will require significant state involvement in developing NPL infrastructure and standards, including in implementing necessary legal reforms for a functioning market or providing fiscal or regulatory incentives to creditors and investors to tackle the NPL issue.

That said, there is no clear-cut reason why publicly owned platforms should operate more efficiently than those owned by private sector operators. State involvement also brings with it a risk of political interference.

In some jurisdictions, which are in the very early stages of development, private operators may be unwilling to risk the cost of establishment until there is greater certainty around how the market will develop. Subject to regulatory permissions and the platform operations being compliant with local law, it may not be necessary to have a physical presence in a specific country to operate in that country's market.

Given political sensitivities, a regional platform (or one which covers more than one specific market) may be better operated by the private sector. Moreover, private operators would bring commercial experience of running a platform and of NPL transactions. Guidelines could be introduced to cover best practice execution and minimum standards to protect against market abuse, should one player become dominant.

Considering their vast experience and that they may already have their own platforms, AMCs could be an option for third-party disposals. As owners of NPLs, this could be perceived as creating a conflict of interest (i.e., that more effort is put into disposing of the AMC's own NPLs as opposed to those owned by third parties—albeit, this could be dealt with in service-level agreements). Moreover, not all countries in the region have their own AMC.

Finally, a platform established and owned by an international or regional development organization could represent another option, at least in the initial stages, with the ownership model evolving over time. This could be beneficial in two ways: (i) from a timing perspective, on the basis that international and/or regional development organizations' cross-government or cross-border connections may help eliminate potential roadblocks; and (ii) in terms of access to funding, with the private sector taking a greater ownership stake once the platform has become established.

Table 14 summarizes the pros and cons of each ownership model.

Table 14: Alternative Ownership Models—Pros and Cons

Ownership	Pros	Cons
Public	Key role in removing roadblocks	Risk of political interference
Private	Commercial know-how and practical experience	Time to develop may act as a disincentive to private sector operators looking for a commercial return.
Public AMCs	Market knowledge	Conflict of interest perception
IDO/RDO	Ability to work cross-border Politically neutral	Level of resourcing required

AMC = asset management company, IDO = international development organization, RDO = regional development organization.
Source: Authors' compilation.

On balance, while private sector ownership may offer a number of practical advantages, there is an important role to be played by individual government and regulator in the early developmental stage, particularly in implementing necessary legal reforms and providing the necessary incentives to buyers and sellers. This could include some form of public–private partnership to overcome potential initial private sector hesitancy, including in terms of the initial funding model. Further discussion on this topic is likely to be needed.

H. Governance

Platforms would need to comply with all appropriate national laws and regulations of the countries in which they operate, including in terms of data protection. Operators will need robust privacy and data confidentiality policies and cyber security protections (firewalls, access monitoring system, document tracking, etc.).

Equally, both domestic and cross-border markets would benefit from the agreement of minimum common standards. Compliance with such standards would earn the platform a seal of approval which could be beneficial in building user confidence. International development organizations could play an important role in this—as standard setter—or by encouraging the establishment of an industry-wide independent standard setter for the region.

Consistent with transaction platforms already in use, an online NPL platform for the Asian region would not provide settlement services or be part of the legal contracting process—all of which would take place off-platform, on a bilateral basis between the parties. Nor would the platform ever "own" the assets.

Dependent on services offered, accredited platforms would be subject to the governance requirements and standards set by the industry body granting the seal of approval.

Further consideration of regulatory requirements is likely to be needed during the planning phase of this knowledge project.

I. Incentives for Using an Online Platform and Other Considerations

Incentives to use the platform. Aside from general incentives for banks to deleverage (e.g., reduced Pillar 2 capital requirements,[8] lower risk-weighted assets, and improved liquidity, among others), online NPL transaction platforms offer potentially significant process benefits, including

- wider and deeper channels to market (as noted earlier, platforms typically maintain lists of potential acquirers of NPL assets and their preferences) and better matching between buyers and sellers;
- faster execution (anecdotally, platform operators speak to between 55% and 90% reduction in times compared to offline processes);
- lower transaction costs; and
- better pricing compared to offline disposals.

From a financial stability perspective, regulators, central banks, and AMCs will be interested in the development of an online transaction platform as a tool to help resolve high levels of NPLs.

Reflecting on the overall financial stability benefits in terms of better information for policymaking, it may be appropriate to consider fiscal incentives for the use of NPL data templates as part of the development of an online platform.

---

[8]   Determined on the basis of the Supervisory Review and Evaluation Process, the Pillar 2 requirement is a bank-specific capital requirement, which applies and covers risks that are underestimated or not covered by the minimum capital requirement (known as Pillar 1). It is legally binding, and compliance failure can be subject to sanctions. (European Central Bank. Pillar 2 Requirement.)

It was noted during this study that a number of public AMCs reported liquidity issues as a limiting factor in performing their policy objectives (i.e., to aid banks' deleveraging). Insofar as NPL transaction platforms accelerate the process for disposals in the secondary markets, they represent a means for AMCs to better fulfill this part of their financial stability mandate.

Fees. These need to be set at a level that makes commercial sense for the platform operator. Fee structures should be transparent and levels affordable to users regardless of size so as not to act as a disincentive to smaller buyers or sellers. Ultimately, low fee levels are only possible with a critical mass of users. Initially, during the ramp-up phase, some level of subsidy or investment may be necessary. Fees are generally paid by the seller.

A typical fee structure may comprise the following elements (based on existing models in use):

- Buyer registration is free of charge to encourage participation.
- Listing fee—payable for listing the portfolio on the platform (paid by the seller).
- Consignment fee—to be paid in case of an acceptance of bid; this may be regardless of whether the deal completes. This is determined by the level of bid accepted (selling price) or is regulated by an individual agreement and is paid by the seller or otherwise as agreed between parties (payable by the seller).
- Data preparation and validation fee (payable by the seller)—This is to incentivize banks to gather high quality loan-level information since loan inception.
- Hosting fee—There could also be a time-based hosting fee to discourage "stale" portfolios being left on the platform unsold for many months, since this would undermine confidence in the platform.

J.   Road Map for the Development of Nonperforming Loan Markets in the Region and an Online Nonperforming Loan Trading Platform

Development of an online platform to trade NPLs in the region, including on a cross-border basis, is a significant undertaking. Not all countries in the region are ready for such an initiative, with potentially significant legal and other reforms necessary beforehand that could take several years to achieve.

The following principles and actions may guide the further development of the NPL market in the region and the development of an online NPL trading platform (Table 15).

As a near-term next step, a broader consultation would be beneficial to include international development organizations (a number of whom are looking at this) as well as relevant central banks and regulators who will have an interest in the macrofinancial and financial stability benefits of the initiative. Central banks and regulators will also have a key role to play in removing roadblocks both to the development of NPL markets, generally, and in terms of NPL online platforms. The inclusion of private sector platform operators would be advantageous to impart lessons learned from practical experience as well as potential users of the platform (holders of NPL stocks and investors) and industry representatives.

Table 15: Key Principles for the Development of Nonperforming Loan Markets and an Online Trading Platform

Principles
Level playing field—To maximize their overall effectiveness, NPL markets and platforms should be regulated on a nondiscriminatory basis, with the same standards and regulatory requirements applying to both foreign and domestic NPL investors.
A level of **minimum standards** should be developed both in terms of NPL markets generally and online NPL platforms.
Balanced protections for consumers—Regulators need to strike a balance between appropriate and sustainable collection practices (which protect consumers and borrowers) and industry standards that do not restrict lenders' ability to efficiently work out NPLs.
NPL markets in different jurisdictions are not all at the same stages of development. As such, **development of a regional platform may best be attempted in stages**, focusing first on those countries that are ready for it, with other countries joining the platform later on.
A **regional network of platforms** could be an alternative to a single regional platform. These would share common standards in terms of best practice operation and information disclosure, and cooperate with each other to maximize reach and the number of transactions.
A precondition for a country joining the platform would be the **adoption of agreed international standards for NPL recognition and valuation methodologies**.

NPL = nonperforming loan.

Source: Authors' compilation.

Areas for further consideration and consultation might include

- development of appropriate best practice guidance for NPL management and disposals—e.g., along the lines of the guidance that the European Commission has announced it is intending to develop in conjunction with the EBA (EC 2020);
- minimum standard setting; and
- harmonized data templates for NPL transactions.

Appendix
List of Partners in the Conduct of Interviews and Survey

A. Interviews Conducted
European Banking Authority
First Financial Network, Inc.
Fund for Problem Loans (Kazakhstan)
International Finance Corporation
Korean Asset Management Company (Republic of Korea)
Sukhumvit Asset Management (Thailand)
Viet Nam Asset Management Company (Viet Nam)
Zheshang Asset Management Company (People's Republic of China)

B. Survey Conducted
China Great Wall Asset Management Company
Debt and Asset Trading Corporation
Fund for Problem Loans (Kazakhstan)
Korean Asset Management Company (Republic of Korea)
Sukhumvit Asset Management (Thailand)
Viet Nam Asset Management Company (Viet Nam)
Zheshang Asset Management Company (People's Republic of China)

Source: Authors' compilation.

References

Asian Development Bank (ADB). 2021a. *Asian Development Outlook 2021 Update: Transforming Agriculture in Asia*. Manila.

———. 2021b. *Asian Economic Integration Report*. Manila.

———. 2022. *Asian Development Outlook 2022: Mobilizing Taxes for Development*. Manila.

Bloomberg China. 2020. Chinese Banks' NPL ABS Issuance in 2020 Sets a Record and Is Expected to Remain High This Year Under the Pressure of Bad Debt Rebounds. 6 January.

European Banking Authority (EBA). 2021. *Discussion Paper on the Review of the NPL Transaction Data Template*. Paris. 4 May.

European Central Bank (ECB). 2020. COVID-19 and Non-Performing Loans: Lessons from Past Crises. *Research Bulletin*. No. 71. Frankfurt.

European Commission (EC). 2020. *Action Plan: Tackling Non-Performing Loans in the Aftermath of the COVID-19 Pandemic*. Brussels.

Financial Supervisory Service (FSS). 2021. Issuance of Asset-Backed Securities 2020. 29 January.

Heppe, B. 2020. *Updated Forecasts of NPL Ratios and Recoveries after COVID-19*. London: NPL Markets Ltd.

Huljak, I., R. Martin, D. Moccero, and C. Pancaro. 2020. Do Non-Performing Loans Matter for Bank Lending and the Business Cycle in Euro Area Countries? *ECB Working Paper Series*. No. 2411. Frankfurt: European Central Bank.

Lee, J., C. Y. Park, D. Park, and P. Rosenkranz. 2021. Strategies for Developing Asia's Nonperforming Loan Markets and Resolution Mechanisms. In J. Fell, M. Grodzicki, J. Lee, R. Martin, C. Y. Park, and P. Rosenkranz, eds. *Nonperforming Loans in Asia and Europe— Causes, Impacts, and Resolution Strategies*. Manila: Asian Development Bank.

Lee, J. and P. Rosenkranz. 2019. Nonperforming Loans in Asia: Determinants and Macrofinancial Linkages. *ADB Economics Working Paper Series*. No. 574. Manila: Asian Development Bank.

McKinsey & Company. 2020. How COVID-19 has Pushed Companies over the Technology Tipping Point—and Transformed Business Forever. Survey. 5 October.

Park, C. Y. and K. Shin. 2020. The Impact of Nonperforming Loans on Cross-Border Bank Lending: Implications for Emerging Market Economies. *ADB Briefs.* No. 136. Manila: Asian Development Bank.

Taobao. 2021. Targeted Marketing (in Chinese).

www.ingramcontent.com/pod-product-compliance
Lightning Source LLC
Chambersburg PA
CBHW042034220326
41599CB00045BA/7381